STARK

# LEKTÜRE ENGLISCH

Rainer Jacob

## Abenteuergeschichten

Mittelstufe

STARK

**Bildnachweis:**
Umschlag: © Philcold | Dreamstime.com; S. 7: Severino Perelda, Studio e Laboratorio d'Arte, Bozen; S. 11: © Linda Bucklin | Dreamstime.com; S. 14: Foto: tagstiles.com/www.photocase.com; S. 24: © Maksym Yemelyanov | Dreamstime.com; S. 35: APA Guide London, Langenscheidt-Verlagsgruppe, Bild: Anthony Howarth; S. 44: Her Majesty Stationary Office, London; S. 54: Porträt: Drawn on stone from a daguerreotype by A. Morhart, New York 1859; Karte: House Divided Project, Dickinson College; S. 67, 72: © Luca Oleastri | Dreamstime.com; S. 79: Getty Images; S. 86: picture alliance/empics; S. 94, 97, 98, 103, 107: Reproduced from Molly K. Bellew: Tales from Tennyson. Illustrator: H.S. Campbell. New York: Jamieson-Higgins Co 1902

ISBN 978-3-89449-294-6


www.stark-verlag.de
1. Auflage 1997

# Inhalt



**Autor:** Rainer Jacob

# Vorwort

**Liebe Schülerinnen, liebe Schüler,**

wir leben in einer Welt, in der es immer weniger Abenteuer gibt. Durch Geschichten können wir dennoch unserem Alltag entfliehen und die Spannung vergangener, gegenwärtiger und zukünftiger Tage erleben.

Begebt euch auf eine unglaubliche Reise: Steigt rund 5 000 Jahre vor unserer Zeitrechnung mit einem Jäger hinauf in die eisige Welt der Berge und Gletscher, reist im fernen Jahr 2189 in einem Raumschiff zu unbekannten Planeten und trefft auf euch feindlich gesonnene Aliens. Taucht nach versunkenen Schätzen und werdet Zeugen, wie üble Gestalten versuchen, die englischen Kronjuwelen zu rauben. In der Erinnerung eines Bodyguards werden die dramatischen Ereignisse um die Ermordung von Präsident Kennedy noch einmal lebendig – und euch erwartet noch einiges mehr …

Die spannenden Geschichten unterhalten nicht nur, sie helfen euch auch, euer Wissen über England und die USA zu vertiefen. Auch die Verbesserung eurer Englischkenntnisse kommt nicht zu kurz. Für ein flüssiges Lesen werden schwierige Wörter auf Deutsch erklärt.
Und jetzt: Viel Spaß beim Schmökern!

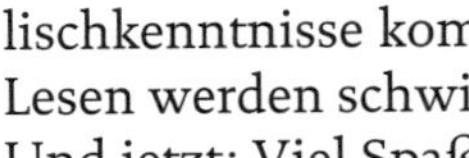

Rainer Jacob

# Ice on Fire

He felt it was getting colder the higher he climbed the mountain. Now and then the sun disappeared behind a dark grey cloud. The first snowflakes started to fall. A cold wind blew them into his face. He was glad his fur[1] coat was a good protection against the wind and the snow. He had taken a long time to hunt the deer and use their skins to make a really warm coat. Now he was glad that he had acted with so much foresight.

He had walked a long way since leaving the dwellings[2] deep down in the valley. Nobody had ever been so high up the mountain before. He would find out what there was on the top of the hill where the sun and the moon lived together. He felt for the little stone in his pocket.

When they were sitting around the big warming fire in the long-house after the hunt the older men told stories about wild elephants and evil spirits. The spirits, they said, lived up on the tops of the mountains. At night they would come out to send down rain or snow into the valley. As a young boy he had always become frightened when he listened to Old Arguru telling the story of the hunter who had seen the

---

1 fur – *Pelz*
2 dwelling – *Wohnplatz*

mammoth[3] in the fire. Old Arguru, who had lost all his teeth, always lowered his voice because he did not want the powerful spirit in the mountain to hear what he was saying.

"My father's father told me about Orgen," he used to begin, "the man who saw the mammoth in flames. For days Orgen followed the small path into the big hills. He went on and on, he climbed higher and higher, until there were no more trees. He camped for the night because he wanted to go on to the top of the mountain the next morning. Hardly had he lain down when he was woken by loud thunder. Flames were coming towards him. At the centre of the raging[4] fire he saw a huge mammoth with two large white tusks[5]. The woolly animal lowered its head and wanted to attack Orgen. He jumped to the side, but there was no more rock or soil – and he fell over the side down the mountain. Fortunately he landed in the trees below. That was where the search party found him. His bones were broken and his hair had become snow-white. Never again did anyone go that high into the mountain!"

But that was just a story. An old men's tale. He was not afraid. Again he touched the small stone disk in his pocket. He felt the encouraging warmth of the little stone. It would give him strength and help him to become a hero among his people. He would prove to

---

3 mammoth – *Mammut*
4 raging – *wütend*
5 tusks – *Stoßzähne*

the others what a bold man could do. Before setting out on his adventure, he had painted blue lines onto his arm to protect him from the evil forces. This tattoo would keep off the ghost of the dark.

He felt hungry and his feet started to hurt. His shoes were stuffed with grass to keep his feet warm. Hinuna had made them for him. She had spent long evenings chewing the leather to make it soft and smooth. His feet were warm still, but the long walk on the rocky ground began to take its toll. Walking through the snow which had become deeper and deeper made him breathe heavily. The cold air hit his lungs. He needed a rest, he needed a place for the night! Arguru would warn him not to go on! A smile flew over his weather-beaten face as he remembered Arguru's words, spoken such a long time ago. What would Old Arguru say if he could see him now!

It was getting darker, the snow fell more heavily now, and the wind had almost dropped completely. The snow reflected the last fading daylight. He knew he would have to find some sort of shelter for the night soon. A careless step in the black night could mean his end. He could feel cold air through his furry coat. Yesterday he had slipped, and falling he had torn his coat on his left side. Luckily, he was able to sew the hole with grass threads[6]. But, still, the grass threads only provided a makeshift[7] repair. That wouldn't last very long. The cold air began to creep through the

6 thread – *Faden*
7 makeshift – *behelfsmäßig*

opening in his coat to find his warm skin. The first stars came out.

He discovered a place for the night. It looked like the entrance to a burrow[8]. Surely, there wouldn't be any animals that high in the mountains. It seemed a dry and safe place to rest and sleep and wait for the morning sun to bring back warmth and life into the white frozen desert. He took his rucksack off his back – a large bag tied onto a wooden frame. That was better! The straps had dug into his skin and flesh. He carefully opened his bag and took out the canister he had made from the bark of a birch tree. Inside the canister he stored the glowing embers[9] of a fire. If it had been for the weight, he would have left the fire down in the valley. But now in the coldness of the night, he was glad that he had taken the effort of carrying the embers into the mountains. He placed the hot ashes on a dry piece of ground, covered them with a few twigs and small pieces of wood – and soon he could feel the comforting warmth of the little flames. He was pleased with himself.

He ate a few berries and some dried mushrooms from his rucksack. Tomorrow he would make it to the top, tomorrow he would find out about the secret of the mammoth in flames. Perhaps he would even –

What was that? He stopped, he didn't dare to breathe. His heart was beating faster! He had heard a sharp crack in the distance. Now it was turning into a

8 burrow – *Bau (von Kaninchen usw.)*
9 embers – *glühende Asche*

deep rumbling noise. He could feel the ground shaking. The noise was getting louder. A thought flashed through his mind: an avalanche[10] – masses of snow racing down the mountainside, burying everything in its way. Luckily, the noise was further away now. He realised with relief that the avalanche came down on the other side of the mountain! His hand felt for the little stone in his pocket. He was safe.

He wanted to doze a little, but a cold wind blew into his burrow. Perhaps there would be a storm tonight! His small fire had gone out, the twigs were probably too damp. When he had fallen down, his rucksack had got wet. He got up and went outside to pile up[11] a wall of snow in front of his cave. The wind was blowing stronger than ever, the snow as falling heavily. His fur coat was soon white. He covered most of the entrance to his cove[12]. On his knees he crept back inside, closing the "snow door" behind him. He tried to make himself comfortable in his tiny den[13], pressing his arms firmly to his body, making himself small and curling up like a dog. It was completely dark. Through the tiny hole in his snow wall he could see thick snow flakes racing through the air.

He touched for his little stone talisman in his pocket. It re-assured him. He was getting tired, he thought of the warm fireplace in Hinuna's hut. A warm glow

---

10 avalanche – *Lawine*
11 to pile up – *auftürmen*
12 cove – *Schlupfwinkel*
13 den – *Höhle, Bau*

started to fill his body from the inside. It seemed to lift him off the ground. He felt much lighter. Was that Hinuna's cooking that he could smell? Obviously, she hadn't forgotten that she had promised to cook his favourite meal – roasted meat! He felt the warm stone disk in his right hand, giving off an inspiring warm glow ...

***

It was a beautiful day for walking: The sun was shining brightly on the white snow of the Similaun glacier. The sky was blue like on the postcard you could buy at all the souvenir shops or at the reception desk in the hotel. Helmut Simon and his wife Angela had set out early today on their walking trip. It was the last day of their holiday in the Tyrolean Alps this year. Helmut stopped. He wanted to wipe the sweat off his forehead with his big red handkerchief.

"Hey, what is that?!" he shouted to his wife.

"What's what?"

"That brown thing over there. Looks like some little girl's lost her doll up here."

He went over to the brown spot he had discovered in the ice. He pushed more snow aside with his heavy boot – and got the shock of his life. That was a man's head! As an experienced walker in the high mountains Helmut knew that every year dead bodies of missing mountaineers were found in the Alps. But this one was different. There was a hole at the back of his skull!

Perhaps that man had been killed and thrown down the glacier[14] or even buried in it! Be it as it may, this was definitely for the police to decide!

The Simons hurried back to a hikers' shelter to report their find. Not knowing whether to inform the Italian or the Austrian police they phoned both. The Italian carabinieri believed the body was that of yet another ill-fated climber, and said, sorry, today they couldn't come anyway. They would come some time later in the week. They had pulled eight bodies from the ice of the Alpine glaciers this year alone!

Mr Simon urged the Austrian police to come at once. "Believe me, I have seen bodies come out of the glacier," he told them over the phone, "but this is nothing

14 glacier – *Gletscher*

like them. Usually bodies that are trapped in the glacier are white and waxy. This one, however, is brown and dried out. I can tell that it is really old."
"All right. We shall send somebody up this afternoon."

Around three o'clock, Austrian policemen arrived by helicopter and started to free the body from the ice. Police officers and scientists took another five days of work to recover the shrivelled[15] body. The Iceman must have been covered by eternal ice for more than 5,000 years. He was holding a strange little stone firmly in his right hand.

15 shrivelled – *zusammengeschrumpft, runzelig*

## Sea of Gold and Silver

As soon as you put your head under the waves you find yourself in a different spectacular underwater world: the noise stops, the colours change, life is different. In the warm, sunlit and clear water you are amidst colourful fish swimming around a white coral reef. In the distance you can watch dolphins and perhaps a huge but friendly whale. That's probably what you have heard about deep-sea diving, at least that's what they tell you in the adverts for tourists to Florida. But the reality can be different. Diving is always fascinating, but it can be dangerous, too. For us it turned out extremely rewarding. It made us into millionaires. I know what I'm talking about.

My love for the sea and my wish to become a diver began when I read Robert Louis Stevenson's novel 'Treasure Island' at the age of 12. The story about a hoard[1] of pirate gold which lured[2] Jim Hawkins and his shipmates on a treasure hunt fascinated me. I wanted to become a diver exploring the sub-sea world, searching for buried treasure! I even made my own first 'hard hat' diving outfit which I used in a mud-bottomed lagoon. However, there were no deep oceans to conquer in the state of Indiana, where I was born.

---

1 hoard – *Hort; gehorteter Schatz*

2 to lure – *anlocken, ködern*

I learned carpentry from my father, while attending High School at Glen Park, Indiana. After school I went to Purdue University, where I studied engineering and then moved to the Californian coast to pursue[3] my main interest in life: diving. I was one of the first people to buy a scuba (short for: self-contained[4] underwater breathing apparatus) unit which was perfected by the French underwater scientist Jacques Cousteau. My dream was to dive for sunken treasure, but you cannot live on dreams alone, so I opened my first dive shop in a small shed where I sold 'breathing' air as well as scuba equipment needed for underwater exploration. Some of the things I offered for sale were my own inventions and developments: for example spear guns and cameras.

***

The first and most valuable real treasure I found was a beautiful, red-haired girl called Dolores. We fell in love at first sight, and when I found out that Dolores was just as enthusiastic about diving as I was, I knew she was the perfect wife for me. We got married and on our honeymoon we went diving on shipwrecks in Florida and the Florida Keys.

Dolores, also called mermaid 'Deo', became my trusted and reliable partner in my diving adventures.

---

3 pursue – *verfolgen*
4 self-contained – *unabhängig, in sich abgeschlossen*

Four children were born to us, our sons Dirk, Kim and Kane, and daughter Taffi. They all became part of our family enterprise.

The shop was selling quite well, and I started a training school for scuba diving. With other divers, I began to explore the California coast for shipwrecks. One day Dolores came up with the exciting suggestion to hunt for sunken treasure in the Caribbean. Of course, I knew that the Straits of Florida which connect the Gulf of Mexico with the Atlantic Ocean was full of Spanish shipwrecks. In the 16th century Spain enjoyed the benefits of a world-wide empire. The Spanish conquistadors[5] had conquered the South-American empires of

5 conquistadors – *(spanische) Eroberer*

the Incas and the Aztecs. Every year, the Spanish silver fleet crossed the Atlantic loaded with treasure from the mines in the American colonies. The galleons laden with riches were tempting[6] targets for pirates such as Francis Drake, Blackbeard and Henry Morgan. They had established Caribbean bases at Saint Christopher's, Jamaica, and Tortuga. Although the Spanish King appointed his best naval officers to guide and protect the treasure fleet, many ships were raided[7] and robbed. Even more vessels sailed into heavy weather and went down in hurricanes.

We studied old sea charts, dreamed of masses of gold, silver, jewels, and other wealth lying somewhere at the bottom of the seas in shipwrecks, just waiting for us to be picked up, making us rich! So many are the ships that went down that we were convinced if we used the right methods we were bound to find at least one wreck full of gold and wealth! We went on several treasure hunting expeditions, but – unfortunately – didn't have much luck.

***

The turning point came in 1963. I met a treasure hunter named Kip Wagner, who had been attempting to salvage[8] remains of wrecks of the Spanish Silver

6 tempting – *verlockend*
7 to raid – *überfallen*
8 to salvage – *(ein Schiff) bergen*

Fleet lost off Florida's East Coast in 1715. Wagner and his crew did not have the right equipment, so they invited me to join them as a partner on a 50 : 50 basis – and my greatest adventure began.

We soon found that diving on the 1715 Fleet shipwrecks was as difficult as any diving we had ever done before. These doomed ships had been wrecked very close to shore where the water was murkiest[9]. Visibility in the shallow[10] water was often zero. I developed a device that, because of its shape, was called a 'mailbox'. Lowered from the vessel stern[11] over the propellers, the 'mailbox' would send a layer of clear water near the surface downward to the bottom so the divers could see. In the spring of 1964, testing of the 'mailbox' did more than bring clear water to the bottom. The 'mailbox' parted the sands and revealed 1,033 gold coins. I can assure you, once you have seen the ocean bottom paved with gold, you'll never forget it! All in all, we recovered more than $ 20 million in treasure from the 1715 Fleet shipwrecks during the 1960s.

By that time we had made treasure hunting our business. My whole family was involved and many divers and other staff worked for me. We were now quite a large 'firm' called 'Treasure Salvers, Inc.' In 1969 I set myself a new target. I wanted to find the possibly richest galleon ever lost off the coast of Florida: the Spanish golden galleon Atocha, lost in 1622.

---

9 murky – *trübe, düster, finster*
10 shallow – *seicht, flach*
11 stern – *Heck*

When I first set my mind on the search for the Atocha I had no idea that it was to become the greatest galleon hunt ever undertaken, that the hunt would demand the greatest personal efforts, that it would take years, and that it would challenge the patience and stamina[1] of my entire crew. Nor could we anticipate[2] that the discovery would be the richest treasure find since the opening of the tomb of the Egyptian pharaoh Tutankhamen in the Valley of the Kings in the 1930s.

The full name of the vessel was Nuestra Señora de Atocha. In the early 1600s the pockets of the Spanish King were empty, so he was desperately waiting for the treasures of his Silver Fleet to arrive from South America. To transport their treasure the Spaniards used a newly designed type of merchant vessel and warship: the galleon. It was a large, 3- or 4-masted ship developed during the 15th and 16th centuries and became the standard vessel of European navies. Galleons were more slender[3] than previous sailing ships. When the Spanish galleons sank off the Florida coast in heavy weather the financial bankruptcy and consequently the decline of the Spanish Empire could not be avoided.

The more I read about the Atocha and her valuable cargo the more excited I became. The general location of the wreck of the Atocha had long been known, but nobody knew its exact site. Day in, day out we

---

1 stamina – *Ausdauer*
2 to anticipate – *vorhersehen*
3 slender – *schlank, schnittig*

searched the sea floor south and westward of the Florida Keys – but in vain. Every morning we shouted at each other "Today's the day!" encouraging ourselves, trying to overcome feelings of despair and frustration. Month after month passed, still nothing, no gold, no sign of the Atocha. Disappointed divers left my crew, new ones full of hope that success wouldn't be far off joined our team. Some maniacs stayed on from beginning to end. There were many people who ridiculed us and thought we were mad. But I refused to give up! I wanted to find that elusive[4] 'lady' Atocha. For years we were out at sea every day working hard under water, convinced that 'Today is the day!' You won't believe it, but it took 16 years of searching until our day arrived!

***

That day, our day, was July 20, 1985. The day my dream came true! At 1:05 p.m. my son Kane climbed aboard our vessel Dauntless. He took off his diving equipment, his face was beaming and he shouted, "We've hit the jackpot!" We had discovered the wreck of the Spanish 440-ton vessel Nuestra Señora de Atocha, which sank off the southern tip of Florida during a hurricane in 1622! We had found the priceless treasure cargo of the fabled lost Spanish galleon Atocha.

---

4 elusive – *schwer erfassbar*

There was enormous joy, relief and satisfaction aboard the ship. Tears of joy ran down my face.

My voice was almost trembling when I radioed the message home to my wife in our office in Florida: "Put away the charts. We've got the treasure load!"

But still it was to take weeks and months to get the treasure of Nuestra Señora de Atocha from the bottom of the sea to the surface. The bulk of its cargo was 47 tons of silver bars. We also found chests of treasure coins, gold, jewels, and unique artefacts[5].

Finding treasures and artefacts lost to the world is only the beginning of the recovery. They must be conserved, studied, restored, recorded and, to share them with the world, exhibited. One of my projects was to operate a treasure museum. In the 1980s, with part of my share of treasure from the Atocha, I bought a huge building in Key West to permanently house the museum. Attached to the museum are a research centre and conservation laboratories. The name of the place is 'Mel Fisher Maritime Heritage Society Museum.' Thousands of people, students, scholars[6] and interested persons come from all over the world to see the cultural and historical treasures that have been raised from oblivion. So why don't you come for a visit, too? Perhaps I might be there, when you arrive. O, by the way, I'm sorry, I haven't introduced myself. My name is Melvin Fisher.

---

5 artefact – *Kunstgegenstand*
6 scholar – *Wissenschaftler*

## To Catch a Thief

"Now, that's it! Enough is enough!" Arthur Bailey, general manager of the ALL-IN-ONE department store chain threw his biro[1] on his desk. He had just finished reading the latest reports he had received from the ALL-IN-ONE store managers in the Midlands. "This scourge[2] must stop!"

The sun was shining brightly into his comfortable room on the top floor of the London ALL-IN-ONE head office. Next weekend would be August Bank holiday, but Bailey wasn't in a friendly mood at all. He lent back in his huge leather chair and put his feet up on his desk – that was the position he preferred when he wanted to think. The company should never have got rid of the good old store detectives! Ever since the board of directors[3] had decided to rely on high-tech security systems incidents[4] of shoplifting had increased. Swinging round in his chair, Bailey stopped right in front of his desk telephone.

He dialled the number of his assistant Dwane Hemmings.

---

1 biro – *Kugelschreiber*
2 scourge – *Plage, Geißel*
3 board of directors – *Aufsichtsrat*
4 incident – *Fall, Vorfall*

"Dwane, would you please come to my office right away. We have a problem."
"Sounds like Apollo 13, Mr Bailey. I'll be with you at once."

Twelve months ago Bailey had chosen Dwane as his assistant from more than seventy applicants for the job. The young man had finished his business studies at the University of Central England in Birmingham with a first class honours degree. His family – Dwane had two younger brothers and a sister – had immigrated from Jamaica years ago and now lived in Brixton. The fact that Dwane was black probably had made him work harder.

"What is the problem, sir?" Dwane asked on entering Bailey's office.

"Mornin', Dwane! More and more goods are disappearing from the shelves of our branches than ever before."

"It's because of the holiday season. When tourists flood the country there's always more stealing from shops than during the rest of the year."

"I know all that. But if our losses are so high now what will they be like at Christmas? 'Cause that's usually the big time for shoplifters!"

"Can I see the figures?"

"Shoplifting has jumped 35 percent in the past four years. We must do something against those long-fingered customers!"

"And employees[5], too," Dwane added.

"Right. Now, Dwane get yourself on the phone to the security companies we use and find out as much as you can about these latest developments. I want to see you back here in my office at 3 o'clock this afternoon. Off you go!"

"Aye, aye, Sir!" Dwane saluted in a slightly mocking manner.

Bailey went back to his papers, moaning and groaning over the figures. Eventually he picked up his phone.

At 3 o'clock sharp Dwane Hemmings reported at Mr Bailey's office. Mr Bailey was not alone. Sir Ralph was there, too. Sir Ralph, that is Sir Ralph Waterston, one of the big bosses of the company, the most influential member of the board of directors. What had he come in for?

Dwane had no time to ponder this question.

"Now, young man. Tell us what you found out. Put Sir Ralph into the picture as to our security precautions."

"I talked to the security people of Sensormatic Electronics. They confirm our findings that shoplifting is on the increase and has become one of the most common non-violent crimes today. Many stores and shops automatically increase prices by as much as 10 percent to cover the losses."

---

5 employee – *Angestellte(r)*

"But this surely cannot be the solution. We must find out why people steal!" Sir Ralph said.

"Sir, the Sensormatic people know why people steal, they also know what sort of people steal. According to their studies there are several categories of shoplifters. First, there are the 'professionals'. They make their living by stealing – very often to their customers' specifications."

"What do you mean?"

"Someone wants a certain stereo set and 'orders' it. Then the professional shoplifter goes out and steals the required product."

"I see. Which other groups are there?"

"Well, there are the people who take things they could easily pay for and perhaps do not even want. These offenders are often emotionally disturbed."

"I can imagine what you mean. Even rich and famous people get into trouble with the police for stealing."

"Remember the young US tennis player Jennifer Capriati? She had to deal with shoplifting accusations, and even an arrest for marijuana possession. As a teenager she was put under such pressure by her ambitious father that …"

"Yes, yes," Bailey interrupted young Dwane's report.

But Dwane was hard to stop. "There's also the Irish singer Sinead O'Connor. I have always liked her music, and I know she had a terrible time when she was young. She watched her parents split up 'quite violently' when she was eight. That was why she turned wild. She was arrested for shoplifting and sent off first to reform school, later to boarding school."

"Alright. Now we all know that you were a fan of Irish pop. But let's get back to our problem."

"Yes, of course. The greatest number of shoplifters are 'amateurs'. Usually, they have little money, few scruples and an intense desire to own luxuries."

"Fine. So much for the psychological side of the problem. What can we do in our situation? Any suggestions from your clever security people?"

"Oh yes, lots and lots!"

***

He very carefully felt for the screw driver and the razor blade[6] in the right-hand pocket of his jacket. I hope I don't cut myself with it right in the middle of the job. That would be rather nasty. The blood would stain the 501 jeans and very soon everybody could tell ... The screw driver was no problem, but it had not been too easy to get hold of a razor blade in his house. His father and his older brother Dwane preferred electric razors. They both hated shaving foam and blades. Perhaps his mother would keep razor blades in her sewing basket, but he hadn't dared to ask her. She would have wanted to know what on earth he needed a razor blade for. Luckily he remembered that his little sister Charmaine had asked for a razor blade some days ago. She had said she needed it for something they did in their arts lessons. And sure enough, on going through her arts

---

6 razor blade – *Rasierklinge*

utensils he had found the blade. He just hoped he would hold it the right way round to cut the tag from the jeans!

***

"As to the security in our stores, sir. Our supplier of electronic security equipment, that is the Sensormatic Electronics Corporation, the people I have just contacted, have done everything possible to deter shoplifting and reduce losses through theft. There is the *electronic article surveillance*[7] (EAS), we also use closed-circuit television (CCTV) and monitoring systems ..."

"Hold on a minute, young man!" Sir Ralph interrupted. "We know all that. For months I myself and the other members of the board worked on the security system for our stores. But as Bailey informs me it doesn't seem to make any difference!"

Bailey rose from his leather armchair. Turning his back to Dwane he went to the window and looked down on the high street. It was a busy Saturday afternoon. The weather was fine, families were out and about – an ideal day for shopping – and stealing.

"If only you could tell a thief from his face, but you can't!" Bailey sighed.

---

7 surveillance – *Überwachung*

"Sir!" Dwane made a fresh start. "They told me about their latest development in anti-theft tags[8]."

"What is that? More expensive high-tech? Expensive and useless?"

***

He was glad that the store was so busy. Parents were trying to do their shopping and keep an eye on their kids at the same time. A few kids were running around and screaming, playing hide and seek. Mothers were shouting. Shop assistants hated this time of the week, most of them looked tired and were probably looking forward to closing time. But 6 o'clock was still more than two hours away! He knew he had enough time.

"Their latest innovation is an 'ink tag'"

"Ink tag? You mean a tag that's got ink inside?"

"Exactly. It's a plastic disk containing three glass vials of indelible[9] ink. The disk is attached to a garment and can be removed only with a special tool. Tamper with the tag and the ink spills, staining the fabric and perhaps a finger or two. Clever, isn't it?" Dwane smiled broadly, waiting for some applause. But that didn't come. Instead Bailey turned to Sir Ralph.

"You know, in some ways I'm rather old-fashioned. We should go back to the more traditional deterrents. Low-tech antitheft systems. Six weeks ago the Tesco

8 tag – *Anhänger*

9 indelible – *nicht entfernbar, wasserfest*

supermarket in Ealing stood life-size cardboard replicas of local police officers next to tempting items such as videos, CD's and cosmetics."

"That's a joke!"

"No. Not at all. The cut-outs cost only £ 500 apiece, but have reduced shoplifting in the store 30 percent in the past six weeks. Tim Nash, the manager there, you know our friend Tim, don't you, ..." Before Sir Ralph could nod Bailey went on with, "Well, Tim tells me 'We don't have to pay them, or give them sickness benefit and holidays, or service them like electrical equipment. We just wipe them over once a week with a damp cloth.'"

***

There were not so many customers in the men's department. He went to the section with exquisite clothing, browsed around and finally picked the most expensive jeans in his size. You were allowed to take three items a time into the changing room to try on. That would be convenient. Inside the cubicle[10] he carefully took out the screw driver and the razor blade and began to remove the tag. Don't cut into the fine cloth, he said to himself. Relax. Easy, you have all the time in the world. It was hard going, but eventually the tag came off. He put on the new jeans, and then his old ones over on top. Wearing two pairs of jeans at the

---

10 cubicle – *Kabine*

same time seemed a bit uncomfortable at first, but he knew he would be alright and make it home. He picked up the other two pairs, pulled the curtain aside and placed these jeans back on the rack[11]. Lots of people were trying on Levi's in various sizes and colours. He heard one mother saying, "I'm not going to pay that much just for a pair of jeans. Why don't you take one from the 'reduced' rack, Kevin?" "But, Mum, they aren't fashionable! None of the kids in my class wear those!" the youngster complained. What a good job his mother wasn't here! He turned round, headed for the escalator to take him down to the first floor and the main entrance. He passed the electronic theft-protection gate without any trouble. He smiled to himself, rather pleased. "Excuse me, young man." Turning round he saw a grey-haired middle-aged man with glasses. "I am the store detective. Would you follow me to my office, please."

***

Sir Ralph looked at Bailey inquiringly. "This is all well and good. But what is your point, Arthur? What are we going to do about it?" Just then the intercom buzzed. It was Bailey's secretary Paulette. "He is here, sir, your undercover man. Do you want to see him straight away?"

11 rack – *Gestell, Regal*

"Yes, please, Paulette. Send him in right now. Thank you."

Sir Ralph looked at Dwane, who shrugged his shoulders as if to say "I don't know what is going on here either!"

Bailey looked rather secretive. He had something up his sleeve. "Hang on a minute, Sir Ralph, and you'll find out what I've been trying to tell you."

The door opened and Dwane saw a bespectacled middle-aged man in a dark suit entering the room. He was holding a teenager by his left arm.

"Why, hey, Tony! What are you doing here?" Dwane wanted to know, surprised to see his younger brother. But before Tony could open his mouth, Arthur Bailey turned to Sir Ralph, pointing at the middle-aged visitor.

"This is George Ellis, store detective, Sir Ralph. He has just caught that young boy red-handed[12]."

"O my God! What!!" Dwane was swallowing[13] hard. He was shocked.

"That's right," the detective said. "He has just stolen a pair of jeans. He took three pairs off the rack, but returned only two. By the look of him, he's put his old pair on top of the new ones, but we'll soon find out, won't we?"

"Tony! Tell me, that this is not true. How could you do this to our family. Haven't you thought about what

---

12 red-handed – *auf frischer Tat*

13 to swallow – *schlucken*

this means to Mum and Dad! What a disgrace!" Dwane had overcome his shock, his face had turned red. He was furious.

"They have worked so hard to give us a better life, and you ...!!"

"But Dwane ..." Tony, however, had no chance of stopping his enraged brother.

"You dirty little thief, you ...!!"

"Stop it, Dwane!" Arthur Bailey's booming voice filled the room. "I'm sorry. It is all my fault."

"I beg your pardon?" Dwane looked puzzled and helpless.

"I'm sorry, Dwane. I asked your brother Tony to help me. I told him to steal a pair of jeans from our store to test our security."

"You did what? You ... Tony? Mr Bailey? I ..."

Poor Dwane didn't know what to say or who to turn to. He wasn't sure if he should shout at Tony or even at Mr Bailey. But in the end relief took hold of him and he sighed.

"Is that true, Tony? Thank goodness!"

Bailey repeated, "I'm sorry, Dwane. Perhaps I should have let you in on it[14]."

Turning to Sir Ralph Mr Bailey then added, "You know very well, Sir Ralph, that last year the board of directors decided to replace all our store detectives with high-tech anti-theft devices. Not one of the directors took any notice of my written objections[15],

14 to let s.o. in on sth. – *jmdn. in etwas einweihen*
15 objection – *Einwand*

and the result has been disastrous! So I thought I'd give them proof that humans are – sometimes – more efficient than machines and gadgets[16]. So, here you are. George observed that boy take three articles, but return only two. Tags would not have caught this thief."

"I can see your point; Arthur, and will advise the board to reconsider its decision. But don't you think your method was a rather drastic one. Especially as far as your assistant is concerned?"

Bailey looked at Dwane, who stood there, half-relieved and half-worried.

"I do apologise, Dwane."

"That's all right, sir. It was just such a shock to see Tony of all people ..."

"I know. But I thought I might ask him to carry out this as a first job for his new employer."

"His new employer? Are you saying that Tony ..."

"That's right. Tony had come to my office, asking for information about a job with our concern. I liked his initiative, I thought that some day he would make an excellent sales manager. But he has to go to university first. Our company will pay for his studies. Do you think that this will be enough compensation for the shock suffered, Dwane?"

"Yes, more than enough. Thank you, sir", Dwane laughed and slapped his brother Tony on his shoulder.

---

16 gadget – *Gerät*

## Dangerous Friends

All day long April showers had come down upon the city. Now as night was descending[1], the rain had stopped, but gusts of wind[2] made walking along Byward Street difficult for a man and a woman hurrying towards the Tower of London. Both were dressed in dark clothes and were wearing hoods over their heads to protect themselves against the wind.

"Damn this bloody weather!" the man shouted through the wind.

"Thomas! Watch your language. You are a parson now, remember?" said the young woman walking behind him.

The man addressed as 'Thomas' looked indeed like a portly[3], middle-aged clergyman[4]. His language, however, was not that of a man who preached the word of God.

"And for Christ's sake, Lilian, how often do I have to tell you not to call me 'Thomas' any more. I am the Reverend[5] Michael Limb now and you are my dear wife Lilian. We are travellers who have come down all

1 to descend – *herabsinken, sich senken*
2 gust of wind – *Windstoß*
3 portly – *beleibt*
4 clergyman – *Geistlicher*
5 Reverend – *Hochwürden*

the way from Loughborough to London to see the Crown Jewels in the Tower of London."

"And a very nervous traveller I am, Thom-, ah Michael! Can you see the Martin Tower over there in the distance?"

"Of course, I can. And I'm definitely just as nervous as you are, Lilian, but don't show it, otherwise the whole operation is off even before it has started."

"I know, and I'll try my very best. But supposing he won't let us in? It is getting rather late!"

The sun which had stayed behind dark low-hanging clouds all day, had now disappeared completely behind the horizon. Daylight was fading fast. It was a nice time of day, really. They called these hours 'the twilight hours'. The people of the city had ended their day's work and were looking forward to bed – or perhaps even to a glass of ale or two in the pub first to round off the day. Everybody that is – apart from thieves and rogues[6] ...

"He'll let us in, I can assure you. I know everything about that old man King Charles II has entrusted with the security of the Crown Jewels."

"Tell me about him again, it makes me feel safer and more at ease!"

"His name is Talbot Edwards, and he is an old man of 77. He lodges above the room where the Jewels are displayed and acts both as caretaker and guide. Instead

6 rogue – *Schurke*

of paying him a salary the King has allowed him to 'show the regalia to strangers' and keep whatever people might pay him in admission fees. As this is Edwards' only source of income, I'm sure he'll readily agree to show us the Crown Jewels. So there! The only thing you have to remember is to faint[7] at the right time and in a way that will convince everybody. Okay?!"

"Okay!"

The wind was still strong, and the rain had set in again. The cobble stones in Mansell Street were shining in the light of the first lamp post the night-watchman had lit. There were few people around. Now and then a stately coach drawn by horses passed by carrying rich and noble people back home to the countryside from the city. The pavements were filthy, full of litter[8] thrown into the streets by busy housewives cleaning their dirty little hovels[9] in this old part of London. A beggar was squatting in the rubbish, holding out his right hand, mumbling at the two passers-by. Thomas kicked him to get passed the wretched[10] creature. The smell of the near-by Thames, the sewer[11] of London, added to the unpleasant concoction of odours[12].

---

7 to faint – *ohnmächtig werden*
8 litter – *Abfall*
9 hovel – *Schuppen, Bruchbude*
10 wretched – *elend*
11 sewer – *Abwasserkanal*
12 odour – *Geruch*

They arrived at the main entrance to the Tower. Two warders in their picturesque Tudor costumes of red and gold stopped the late visitors. People had started to call them 'Beefeaters' as meat from the King's table was a regular part of their diet. The watchmen inquired what the clergyman and his wife wanted, told them then to hurry up and showed them the way to the Martin Tower.

***

A knock at the door – and a head appeared above in a window.

"Who's there?"

"Good evening. We would like to see the Crown Jewels."

"At this time of day?! It's a bit late for that. Come back tomorrow!"

"That's old Edwards all right", Thomas whispered to the young lady standing behind him, and in a loud voice he added, "Forgive us, sir, for troubling you so late, but my wife and I have had a long journey down from the Midlands. Outside Nottingham our coach broke down and we had to wait for hours in the rain. Would a few extra coins compensate[13] you for your trouble?"

The old man's voice changed to a more mellow and welcoming tone.

---

13 to compensate – *entschädigen*

"All right, I'll be down in a minute."

"Pull yourself together – and stop shaking!" Thomas hissed under his breath to Lilian.

The old man had made his way down the creaking staircase. His grey hair was all over his face, so that you could hardly see his small wrinkled eyes. He opened his mouth to display a few stumps of dark brown teeth: "Now then, vicar. If it weren't for the church, I would have sent you away tonight. But as I'm a believer in God ..."

"Yes, yes," the clergyman interrupted the old man's ramblings. "Here is some money for your troubles. Could you now please show us the Crown Jewels?"

The keeper, who carried a torch in his left hand, led them to the heavily bolted door, turned a big key in the iron lock and asked his visitors to step inside a dark room. He locked the door behind them as regulations demanded. And there it was! – glittering in the light of the torch: the treasure Thomas Blood had dreamed of so long!

"Are you all right, lady?" old Edwards asked when he saw the young woman leaning on to the wall and sighing[14] deeply.

"O yes, I think I am, it's just that ..." But she could not say any more. With her back to the wall she let herself slide down onto the floor, her eyes closed.

"Sir! Sir! Your wife! I don't think she's well," the keeper of the Crown Jewels exclaimed looking for the parson who had disappeared behind one of the glass showcases.

The parson went down on his knees to hold his wife's hand. "O dear, the long day we've had has proved too much for her. And the sight of so much gold and jewellery must have given her the rest."

"Wait here. I'll call my wife for help," said the old man.

As soon as Edwards had left the room the young woman opened her eyes.

"What now?!"

---

14 to sigh – *seufzen*

"Stay down there where you are and try to remember as many details of the room as possible. I'll do the same. When the old bloke is back, we'll leave like normal visitors."

"Why don't we take the Jewels right now?"

"Don't be stupid, woman. I've told you more than once: we are preparing the theft of the century, we are not carrying it out today. That will take more than just two people!"

At that point the guardian came back with his wife. Mrs Edwards quickly held some smelling salts under Lilian's nose. The old couple then invited the sick woman and her husband into the house to recover properly.

"I am very grateful for everything you have done for us. May God bless you!" the vicar said, holding his wife's arm and getting ready to leave.

"Nice people," thought Talbot Edwards, turning to his wife, completely unaware of the fact that they had just met two of the people who were about to commit the most daring theft of the age: the stealing of the Crown Jewels from the Tower.

Instead, on that April day in 1671 Edwards watched a middle-aged clergyman and his wife disappearing into the dark night.

***

Talbot Edwards, the guardian of the Crown Jewels, and his wife could not know that they were about to become the victims[15] of a cleverly worked out plan. The man whom they had got to know as a clergyman was not a man of God at all. His real name was 'Colonel' Thomas Blood, born in Ireland in 1618, the son of a blacksmith. His life had been a dramatic one: He started out as a loyal defender of the King, later a supporter of Parliament and eventually turned into one of the most infamous[16] rogues of the Restoration in the 17th century. In the Civil War Blood had first risked his life fighting bravely for the cause of the King. Then, however, he changed sides. When the war came to an end, he was rewarded for his courage and support of Parliament by Cromwell. In recognition of his bravery he was made a Justice of the Peace and given a piece of land. Until 1660 he lived quietly, enjoying the fruits of his hard won prosperity. But his life was changed completely by the Restoration, when the new rulers took his land from him and destroyed his home. Out of anger and frustration Thomas Blood turned to a life of crime and insurrection[17]. He was involved in many of the plots which disturbed England in the early years of the reign of Charles II. A master of disguise[18], Thomas Blood constantly avoided being caught. He moved swiftly around the country, causing unrest wherever

15 victim – *Opfer*
16 infamous – *berüchtigt*
17 insurrection – *Aufstand*
18 disguise – *Verkleidung*

he went. Now, after eleven years of adventure, he was ready to attempt the most daring crime of his career: the theft of the Crown Jewels.

***

The first step in Blood's audacious[19] plan was to win the confidence and trust of the old guardian of the Jewels, Talbot Edwards. Therefore, several days after the faked fainting of the parson's wife Thomas Blood disguised himself again as clergyman and returned to the Martin Tower with a present of four pairs of white gloves for Mrs Edwards, who was delighted and touched by the gift. On that occasion Blood met Alice, the daughter of the old couple, for the first time. He noted with great interest that Mrs Edwards was rather worried that Alice had not yet met the right man to marry. And as she wasn't getting any younger ...

When the parson eventually left, Mr and Mrs Edwards told the clergyman that he was always welcome in their home and to call again whenever he liked. Blood took advantage of the recent developments and adapted[20] his plan to the new circumstances.

---

19 audacious – *verwegen, waghalsig*
20 to adapt – *anpassen*

***

Two days later, the clergyman knocked at the Edwards' door again.

"Oh, hello, Reverend Limb. It's nice to see you. Do come in, please," Mr Edwards led their guest, whom they had got to know well by now – they thought – into their small living room right above the room where the Crown Jewels were stored. 'Colonel' Blood's thoughts often wandered down a floor whenever he was visiting the Edwards – thinking of the jewels, gold, and silver below, but he was careful enough never to mention the room full of treasure on his visits to the Martin Tower.

"Where is your lovely Alice?" the clergyman inquired.

"She's in the kitchen, preparing the evening meal."

"Good. Then we won't be disturbed."

"What do you mean?" old Edwards wanted to know.

"Can you keep a secret, Mr and Mrs Edwards?"

"Of course we can. How can you ask, vicar. I have not been made keeper of the Crown Jewels for nothing!" Talbot Edwards said in a proud voice.

"Well, then. I have a nephew about the same age as Alice. And ever since I've seen your lovely Alice I have thought ..."

"Do you mean they would make a happy couple?" Mrs Edwards was livelier now than the 'Reverend' had ever seen her. Her cheeks burning, Mrs Edwards bent forward as if she wanted to make sure that she would not miss a single word of what that nice and friendly vicar was about to tell them.

"Exactly. I think they would make a perfect match. So how can we arrange a meeting between the two young people?"

"Oh, that's no problem." Mrs Edwards took the initiative. "Do come round next Saturday at 7 o'clock with your nephew and let us have dinner together. Bring a few more friends if you like." The Edwards were delighted with the prospect[21] of a suitable[22] husband for their daughter. On the other hand, Blood was more than pleased that the suggestion of a meeting had come from the Edwards themselves and that it fitted into his plans better than he could ever tell them.

***

Saturday, May 9th, was a nice early summer's day. At 7 o'clock it was still light, the air balmy[23], filled with the scents[24] of thousands of flowers that were in full bloom in the Royal Gardens of the Tower. Thomas Blood, wearing his priestly robes, and three companions were on their way to the Martin Tower: The three were Tom Hunt, Richard Hallowell and Richard Parrot. Each of them knew what he had to do. Hunt was to

---

21 prospect – *Aussicht*
22 suitable – *passend*
23 balmy – *lau, mild*
24 scent – *Duft*

play the nephew. Blood had gone through his plan with them dozens of times. He even rehearsed how to overpower the guardian once they had been let into the room with the Crown Jewels. More than once Blood had told them to be careful with Edwards as he was 77 years old already to prevent any serious injury. He realised he felt closer to the old couple than he really should. But, still, he also knew that his companions were a rather violent lot, and you could never tell what they were up to once they were engaged in a fight. Under their black coats each was armed with a sword stick, a dagger[25] and a pair of pocket pistols.

***

From his window on the top floor Talbot Edwards could see the clergyman and his three friends approaching the Tower. His wife had told him to have a look-out and give her a shout as soon as he saw them, because she was hardly able to contain her curiosity about the prospective son-in-law.

"They are here, Betsy!"

Edwards and his wife went down to the front door to greet their guests. Blood introduced his 'nephew' Tom and his two companions, with Mrs Edwards having a discrete but close and inquisitive[26] look at the parson's

25 dagger – *Dolch*
26 inquisitive – *neugierig*

nephew. She was delighted. At least as far as his looks were concerned he had turned out to her satisfaction.

"Mr Edwards, unfortunately my wife has been held back a bit by the arrival of a relative from the Midlands at our quarters. But she'll join us very soon. I have told my three friends here about the marvels of the Crown Jewels. May I perhaps suggest that to pass the time while we are waiting for my wife's arrival we have a look at the wonderful treasure."

"Sure." Talbot Edwards was delighted that he could please his visitors and readily agreed to the suggestion. His wife went back into the house to join her daughter in the kitchen. Edwards was in no way suspicious[27] and did not realise in what danger he was: it was four against one. He carried no weapons whatsoever. He unlocked the door to the Jewel room, let in his guests and stooped[28] to lock it again from the inside according to regulations.

As he did so Richard Parrot roughly seized him from behind. Tom Hunt left the room to keep watch outside. The villains threw a cloak[29] over Talbot Edwards' head and pushed a wooden plug into his mouth to make sure the old man would not make a noise or shout for help.

"Not so rough, you idiots!" Blood shouted.

But Richard Hallowell was already tying up Edwards' hands behind his back.

---

27 suspicious – *misstrauisch*
28 to stoop – *sich bücken*
29 cloak – *Umhang*

"Don't say a word and you won't get hurt!"

A groan came from the guardian's mouth.

"Shut up!" Hallowell bellowed. The old man continued to struggle against his assailants[30], putting up as much resistance as he could. Parrot could not take any more. He knocked the old man over the head with a wooden mallet[31], pulled his dagger from under his coat and stabbed Edwards in the stomach. The old guardian sank to the floor, with blood trickling from his body. Thomas Blood realised that he wasn't able to stop the villainy of his gang, so he tried to divert their attention from the keeper's body to the Crown Jewels. "Hey, lay off!! Remember what we are here for. The Jewels!"

30 assailant – *Angreifer*
31 mallet – *Hammer*

Hallowell and Parrot, believing Edwards was now dead, broke open the showcase in which the Crown Jewels were kept. While Parrot stuffed the orb[32] down his breeches[33], Blood crushed the crown because he found it too big to hide inconspicuously[34] beneath his cloak. Hallowell began to file the sceptre in two.

There was a knock at the door.

"Hey! Somebody is coming!" Tom Hunt shouted from outside.

"What! Can't be!"

"What shall I do? He's coming right up to me!"

"Perhaps he's a late visitor who wants to see the Crown Jewels. Tom, tell him to go away and come back tomorrow! Quiet now – don't make a single sound!"

***

The three men inside the Jewel room kept quiet and listened to how Tom would manage to get rid of the stranger who had by now arrived at the Martin Tower.

"Good evening!" they heard the newcomer say to Tom.

"Good evening, sir. I'm afraid it's too late to see the Crown Jewels tonight. You'll have to come back tomorrow."

---

32 orb – *Reichsapfel*
33 breeches – *Kniehose*
34 inconspicuously – *unauffällig*

"I've seen the Jewels more than once. I'm not interested in them."

"What do you want then?"

"I beg your pardon! What has it all got to do with you? Who are you anyway?"

"My name is Harry Paull. I'm the son-in-law of the guardian of the Crown Jewels and therefore I have every right to ask you for your intentions," replied Tom Hunt.

"And I, my dear friend, have every right to come here to visit my parents!"

"What, ah, I'm sorry, I've ..." Hunt was lost for words. He was completely taken by surprise.

So was Thomas Blood and the other two thieves when they heard these words.

"Blood, you never told us the old fool had a son!" Parrot swore under his breath.

"He told me his son was far away fighting with the English army in Flanders!" Thomas Blood whispered. "Shut up now!"

They listened to what the young Edwards was asking Tom outside.

"Ah, then you're my brother-in-law! Where are my parents, and where is Alice?"

Tom Hunt had recovered from his shock: "They are all upstairs. I was just checking everything was locked up for the night."

"Alright, I'll go in then to give them a nice surprise. I'll see you later."

"You do that."

As soon as the young Edwards had disappeared into the house climbing the stairs to the lodgings of his parents, Blood dropped the sceptre.

"Quick! Quick! Take what you have got and – let's get out of here!"

They left hurriedly with what they had already gathered together and were met by Tom outside.

"We must get out of the Tower as quickly as possible, before the young Edwards and the rest of the family realise what's going on."

At that moment their blood froze. A shrill cry filled the air: "Treason[35]! Murder! The Crown is stolen!" That was old Talbot Edwards' voice! Obviously he wasn't dead and must have been able to remove the gag from his mouth.

***

The chase[36] was on! Thomas Blood and his three accomplices tried to get out of the Tower compound as quickly as possible.

"Run as fast as you can! We'll meet at St. Katharine's Gate by the horses!"

---

35 treason – *Verrat*
36 chase – *Jagd, Verfolgung*

Holding on to the loot each of them had hidden under his cloak, they ran in the direction of the Byward Tower.

There was more shouting and crying behind them. The young Edwards must have taken up the pursuit[37]!

"Hold the thieves! Murder! Treason!"

The Yeoman Warder at the gate, alarmed by the noise and shouting, saw three men running towards him. There's something wrong here, he thought. He stepped in the way of the four men and tried to stop them with his halberd.

"Hey you! Stop! Who are you?"

"Get out of my way, you bastard!" Blood took out his pistol and fired a shot at him.

***

The guard on the drawbridge feared for his life when he saw the Yeoman fall to the ground. He was so frightened that he dropped his musket and let the gang pass. The robbers managed to leave the Tower and then ran along Tower Wharf towards St. Katharine's Gate. But, still, Blood soon realised that their chances of making a get-away had dropped to nil. There were too many people walking along the waterfront! Alarmed by the shouts of the young Edwards and more guards coming from the Tower who had joined

---

37 pursuit – *Verfolgung*

him in the chase, courageous young men stepped intc the way of the thieves and blocked their escape.

Parrot was the first to be seized[38] by two guards. He was still holding on to the orb and the Black Prince's ruby[39], which he had broken off from the sceptre. Then Blood himself was eventually captured after putting up a heavy struggle. He fought so violently against his pursuers that none of them noticed that the crown itself had fallen out from beneath Blood's cloak! For some time the Crown of England lay unnoticed in the gutter[40].

Hallowell jumped into the Thames and tried to swim to safety. But to no avail, he, too, was captured. Hunt was the only one to reach the horses and made off. Unfortunately for him, in his haste he rode into a projecting cartpole[41] in one of the narrow streets near the Tower, fell off his horse and was arrested.

The thieves had all been captured and the Jewels recovered and safely returned into the custody[42] of Gilbert Edwards, who had taken over from his father Talbot as Keeper of the Jewel House.

---

38 to seize – *ergreifen*
39 ruby – *Rubin*
40 gutter – *Rinnstein*
41 cartpole – *Deichsel*
42 custody – *Obhut*

## Greed for Gold

### THE EDINBURGH STANDARD (Es) INTERVIEWS CAPTAIN JOHN AUGUSTUS SUTTER (THE EMPEROR OF CALIFORNIA)

ES: Mr Sutter, we have heard many stories about the Californian Gold Rush in Europe, too. We also know that you were right at the centre of it. That's why my paper has sent me to get first-hand information for our readers back at home. To begin with, Mr Sutter, would you please tell our readers something about your origins.

SUTTER: Well, as you probably know I was born in Switzerland, in Kandern on February 23, 1803, and when I was 36 I thought of making a new life in California.

ES: There are rumours that you went to America to escape from your creditors[1].

SUTTER: It is a little embarrassing to talk about all this, but I promised you I'd be honest. What you have heard is quite right. I owned a store, but business was not going at all well. To be true, it was a complete failure. I ran into heavy debt[2] – and in order to avoid being put in prison I stole aboard a ship to America.

---

1 creditor – *Gläubiger*
2 debt – *(Geld-)Schuld*

ES: Is it true that you abandoned[3] your family, your wife and children?

SUTTER: Yes. I'd rather not talk about this very personal matter. It still hurts me to think about what I did to them.

ES: When you arrived in July 1839 there was no state of California.

SUTTER: Nowhere near. What we now call California was then a neglected Mexican province that had remained pastoral[4] for decades. San Francisco was just a small coastal village with a makeshift landing on the Sacramento River.

ES: How did you start?

SUTTER: After arriving I acquired a land grant from the Mexican government.

ES: How did you manage that?

SUTTER: Well, I wanted to found a new colony, a new place for people who were willing to work and farm the land. California was empty in those days, but I was certain that thousands would eventually want to settle in this fertile part of the world. My dream was to found a new and better Switzerland – New Helvetia I wanted to call it –, a place for refugees in search of new opportunities.

ES: And to immigrants into an up to then empty country was quite in the interest of the Mexicans, wasn't it?

---

3 to abandon – *im Stich lassen*

4 pastoral – *ländlich*

SUTTER: Of course, it was. The land they gave me was at the back of beyond where no one lived – apart from a few natives who didn't count anyway. So with a couple of helpers and adventurers I had hired in San Francisco I travelled the Sacramento River upstream, and where it meets up with the American River we built a fort.

ES: Which later became known to everyone as Sutter's Fort, now the town of Sacramento.

SUTTER: Right. I was not a farmer, though, I was a storekeeper, a businessman. I knew that the newcomers would need lots of things – food, tools, clothing etc. and I was there with my store, ready to sell important supplies to the new influx[5] of residents.

ES: You were more successful than back in the old days in Switzerland, weren't you?

SUTTER: Definitely. Unlike my previous business in Switzerland, the colony soon prospered. Within eight years I had more than one thousand people working for me. Among my employees were also various groups of Mormons, Indians and Mexicans. Young man, I owned 12,000 head of cattle, 2,000 horses and mules, more than 10,000 sheep, and 1,000 hogs. And where is it all now? It makes me sad and furious when I think back to what became of that fertile paradise of mine!

---

5 influx – *Zustrom*

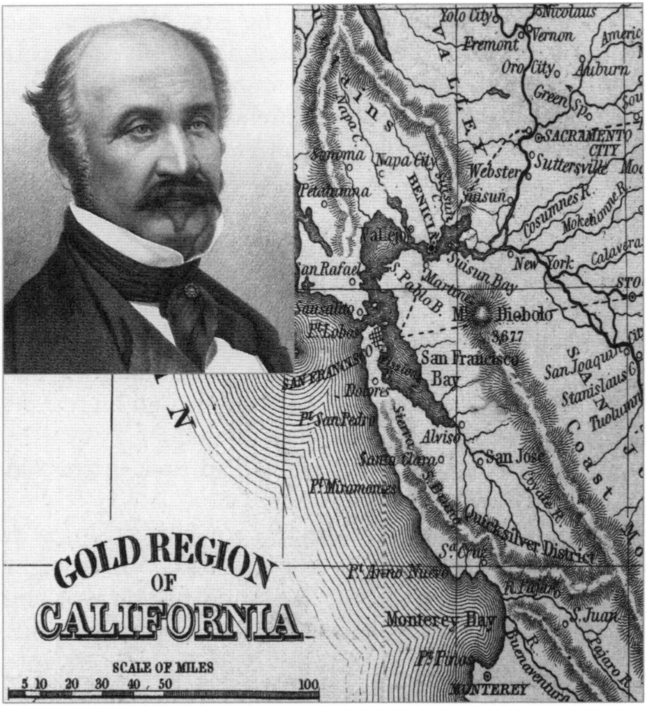


Es: This is exactly what our readers would like to know. What went wrong?

Sutter: It all happened on a Monday in January 1848, Monday 24th to be precise. Gold was found, but I only heard about the discovery four days later.

Es: So Monday, January 24, 1848, was the day when the first gold nugget was found on your land?

SUTTER: That's right. I had started a mill project in Coloma. A saw mill was needed in the area because the valley there is surrounded by fine stands of tall timber. I chose James Marshall as the foreman of the work group to build the mill.

ES: What sort of man was James Marshall, had he been working for you long?

SUTTER: He was quite a character! He was a carriage-maker by trade and came from New Jersey. I first met him in 1845 when I gave him a job as a general utility man. All in all, he was a good worker. Maybe he held strange views about the world at large, but most of the men who worked under him thought he was a pleasant enough fellow. I never had any difficulties with him.

ES: Do you know where he is now?

SUTTER: I am not quite sure, but I think he's in a sad state now. I was told that after the gold find he grew increasingly sullen[6] about his lot. He felt he deserved greater recognition for what he had discovered. As far as I know he spends most of his money on alcohol.

ES: Let's go back to the construction of the mill and the first gold that was found.

SUTTER: Well, work on the mill was almost completed, when Marshall found that the water flowing through the tailrace[7] was backing up. The waterwheel could not turn properly. To solve this problem the tail-

---

6 sullen – *verdrossen*
7 tailrace – *Mühlgerinne*

race had to be deepened to increase the flow of water and thereby create a stronger force to turn the wheel.

ES: Does that mean that the men dug a deeper channel?

SUTTER: Exactly. During the day the men deepened and widened the race. Marshall had the idea to raise the gate every evening and let the water from the river wash out as much sand and gravel[8] as possible. So at night the river did some of the work for the men. In the morning, while the men were getting breakfast, Marshall would shut off the water, and look along the race to see if any further digging needed to be done.

On the cold morning of January 24, Marshall did his usual round. The action of the water had washed away more sand and rocks and he noticed something glimmering in the mud and took a closer look! It was gold! A few glittering flakes of gold!

ES: Did Marshall know that he had struck gold?

SUTTER: I'm sure he did, because he ran back to the mill, shouting, 'Boys, by God, I believe I have found a gold mine!' Of course, the men thought it was another one of Marshall's odd ideas, so they tested the material on the spot – it was bitten, hammered and compared to a $ 5 gold piece. Some still expressed their disbelief, but Marshall was convinced, 'I know it to be nothing else but gold', he said.

ES: Did the men leave the building of the mill alone then and start looking for gold instead?

---

8 gravel – *Kies*

SUTTER: By no means. They carried on as usual. The fever had not broken out at that point.

ES: Mr Sutter, when did you first hear about the gold?

SUTTER: As I told you before, it was four days later. On January 28, 1848, Marshall returned to the Fort for more supplies and immediately asked to see me in my private office. I thought it a bit strange when he insisted on locking the door behind. When he was sure we were alone, he pulled out of his pocket a white cotton rag. Opening the cloth he held it out to me. It contained about an ounce and a half of gold-dust, flaky and in grains, the largest piece not quite so large as a pea. 'I believe this is gold, Captain,' Marshall said to me, 'but the people at the mill laughed at me, and called me crazy.'

ES: Were you able to tell whether Marshall had found real gold?

SUTTER: Not straight away. He might have found some placer gold[9]. So I said to him, 'Well, it looks like gold; but let us examine it more thoroughly.' I owned a copy of the American Encyclopaedia, and with information from the book we tested the nugget with aqua fortis and then checked the specific gravity of the yellow metal. The stuff stood the test. Looking at Marshall for some time I finally said, 'I believe this is the finest kind of gold I have ever come across.'

9 placer gold – *Seifen-(Wasch-)gold*

ES: Did you realise then that the find would change not only your life but also the lives of millions of people?

SUTTER: Oh no, not really. But I had the vague feeling that the gold could be some sort of menace to my paradise. That is why I told Marshall it would be in our best interest to keep the discovery secret. Neither of us wanted strangers wandering about the countryside, claiming the land, and disrupting work on the mill. I said to Marshall he should also instruct the workers to keep the discovery secret until the mill was finished, which they agreed to do.

ES: Did it work?

SUTTER: Of course it didn't. The cook of the work group by the mill, Jennie Wimmer, gave a piece of gold she had found in the riverbed to a supplier who had come along delivering food. Upon returning to the fort, that man used the gold to buy some brandy and soon the whole fort knew about the gold. Gold is a hard secret to keep and within days of the discovery the news began to spread like a wild fire.

ES: I believe the press played an important part in this as well, didn't it?

SUTTER: That is correct. The first printed notice of the discovery was in the March 15 issue of "The Californian" in San Francisco. I have the cutting here. You can read it if you like – my eyes have got a bit weak and tired.

ES: It says here: 'GOLD MINE FOUND: In the newly made raceway of the Saw Mill recently erected by Captain Sutter, on the American Fork, gold has been found in considerable quantities. One person brought thirty dollars worth to New Helvetia, panned[10] there in a short time. California, no doubt, is rich in mineral wealth, great chances here for scientific capitalists Gold has been found in almost every part of the country.'

SUTTER: A few weeks later a man arrived in San Francisco, waving a bottle full of gold in the air, and shouting, 'Gold! Gold! Gold from the American River!' Gold fever struck and within days the city was nearly empty. The publisher of the Californian suspended publication of the paper on May 29 as there were no readers left in town. He, too, went up into the mountain to have a look around for gold himself! The whole country, from San Francisco to Los Angeles and from the seashore to the Sierra Nevada, resounded with the cry of 'Gold! Gold!' People neglected everything, they left their fields half planted and their houses half built. The Gold Rush was in full sway.

ES: What was the situation like in your colony?

SUTTER: I had a look for myself and I found everything abandoned. Mills were idle, crops left untended, houses empty. In almost every stream and river I saw men working with pans and rockers[11], standing knee deep in icy water under the blistering summer sun.

ES: Did you profit from the Gold Rush as well?

SUTTER: At first I did. Immediately after news of the gold discovery broke my business prospered even

10 to pan – *mit einer Goldwäscherpfanne auswaschen*
11 rocker – *Schwingtrog zur Goldwäsche*

more than it had done previously. At the end of the day, all of my supplies were sold. The goods that I supplied were in such high demand that I was able to charge exorbitant prices for them. They would still disappear off of the shelf as fast as we could unpack them. But that was just a flash in the pan[12].

ES: What do you mean by that, Sir?

SUTTER: Deep inside I knew that my dream was ruined. I tried to find ways to profit from the discovery, but my agricultural empire soon began to fall apart. Thousands of gold seekers squatted[13] on my land, and I received nothing in return.

ES: But it was your land, wasn't it? So the gold should really have been yours.

SUTTER: Legally things weren't that clear. There were no real contracts which had made me the owner of the land. I fought for my rights, but in vain. How can you stem a flood? The colony was just overrun by prospectors. Squatters camped in my fields. At first the only people who came to look for gold were men from the coastal towns and ranches, sailors whose ships had brought cargo to San Francisco, or soldiers with no jobs and nowhere to go after the Mexican War. Only the best equipped brought tents. Most settled in brush shelters or just laid out their blankets on the ground. Marshall tried to keep them away from the mill and his

---

12 a flash in the pan – *Strohfeuer*
13 to squat – *sich (unrechtmäßig) niederlassen*

own claims, directing them up and down the river and to tributary streams. But to no avail[14].

Es: You say that your foreman Marshall had his own claims. Did all your workers leave you?

SUTTER: Yes, that was the biggest disappointment. I had given my men and their families a new home, a new start. They had a good life and a bright future ahead. But they threw all that away for a couple of glimmering flakes of gold. I lost most of my employees to the mines. They all wanted to try their hand at gold prospecting. It is true, I got my wheat harvested, but there was no one to thresh it. The stone wheels of my new grist[15] mill never produced any flour. Hides[16] rotted in my tannery vats[17]. Very soon, my fort, Sutter's Fort, was left with no one to work it, worse still, the fort was vandalised for boards and useful bits of ironwork, shovels and pickaxes. It was hell. I hated the people, they destroyed everything for gold!!

Es: Sir, I think our readers can understand the way you feel about all that. But didn't the Gold Rush have a positive effect for the state of California?

SUTTER: This may be true. From the thousands of mining camps emerged the state of California. It emerged out of the dirt and greed, out of the frenzy[18] and madness, which came to an end when the surface

14 to no avail – *nutzlos*
15 grist – *Mahlgut*
16 hide – *Tierhaut*
17 tannery vat – *Bottich in der Gerberei*
18 frenzy – *Raserei*

deposits were exhausted. By 1864 the Gold Rush had ended. The plantations, my plantations, were totally ruined. The rich farmlands were flooded and buried under mud, rocks, and sand. The state of California could have emerged from my colony New Helvetia, much better, much stronger, and with less pain for the country and the people. But when it comes to gold or dollars, people are blind. I shall never forgive them for what they did to me!

ES: Mr Sutter, thank you very much for this interview.

***

P.S.: Two years after this interview, John Augustus Sutter, the man who had started an empire and who had lost all of his wealth, died bitter and disappointed in Washington on June 18, 1880.

## Diary of Astronaut Dave Vandenberg Aboard Starship Equity

**Stardate:** 2189-02-12

At last! After weeks and months of speeding through space at highest PAV (planet-approach-velocity) we have reached our operating position. Everybody on board is happy that the long and boring traverse to sector 17258 in the Galilee zone is over. At 18:23 we reduce speed and enter on a fly-by-course.

No spacecraft from Earth has previously explored the planets in this distant Galilee zone. Our mission is to scan the planets in the area, and if any signs of life are detected the spaceship will remain in orbit[1]. Then our observation and exploration mission can really begin. This is my first trip into the outer regions of the Galaxy – and I am thrilled by the new experience. My friend Angus, whom I first met at the Space Aviation Academy, is just as excited as I am. We both hope that we'll be offered a chance to join an on-surface-expedition – if ever there is need of one.

**Stardate:** 2189-02-13

There will be an on-surface-expedition, and very soon, too! Our scanning devices[2] have detected the existence

1 orbit – *Umlaufbahn, Kreisbahn*
2 device – *Gerät*

of oxygen and methane in the atmosphere and infrared signature from the solid areas of planet 19/8756-3879. Our chief science officer has named it Pelleus X. Radio emissions from the planet, however, are difficult to attribute[3] to natural causes. The signals offer no reliable[4] proof of intelligent life. The captain has ordered an exploratory patrol team. Angus and I are amongst the crew chosen by the First Officer! We shall set out in eight hours.

**Stardate:** 2189-02-14

Scientists have briefed[5] us on conditions on Pelleus X – according to data collected by our scientists up to now. It is hard to believe that there might be life, as we know it, on the planet. A day on Pelleus X is only 9 hours and 48 minutes long. Such fast rotation causes it to be somewhat squashed due to centrifugal force: its polar radius is 4,000 km less than its equatorial radius (the latter being 71,392 km). That means humans weigh almost 25 % more at the equator than at its poles! So a 100 pound person (on Earth) weighs 230 pounds at the planet's equator, but 285 pounds at the pole! This shouldn't worry us too much, as the weight-equalizing device WED-809 of our space suits will compensate[6] that. The suit will also protect us against extreme temperatures and high radiation levels. Tem-

---

3 to attribute – *zuordnen*
4 reliable – *verlässlich*
5 to brief (s.o.) – *(jmdn.) informieren, instruieren*
6 to compensate – *ausgleichen*

peratures on the planet may range from –220 to +220 degrees Celsius. The radiation dose per minute absorbed during our mission will be equivalent to what the average person receives in a whole year on Earth. More dangerous than this, though, could be the dust storms that now and again originate from the planet, our science staff warn us!

**Stardate: 2189-02-15**

We have made our way to the patrol shuttle. There are four team members, – Commander Phil Kerry, Lieutenant Angus MacPherson and I, plus the android robot assistant Jules. The time is reset to Zero Operation Time.

**00:05 in mission**

The auto pilot is programmed to take us down to position 34° north 49° west of square 2-89, the landing site being close to the place from where the radio signals seem to be coming. "Let's go!" Docking off from the Equity, our descent begins. All systems are working perfectly.

**00:13 in mission**

"Shuttle 01!" Captain Sandrew's voice is coming over loud and clear on the intercom from the Equity. "Lieutenant Kerry! Report position! Why are you leaving your programmed trajectory[7]!"

---

7 trajectory – *Flugbahn*

"Sir, according to our instrument readings we are following the set course!"

"No! You are embarking on a course to the moon of Pelleus X, not to its surface! Switch off your autopilot immediately! There must be some interference[8]! I'll talk you down!"

What is interfering with our system? Are we getting incorrect readings on our computer screens? We are not receiving radio signals from Pelleus X any more!

**00:21 in mission**

We are in the entry region of Pelleus X. It is much drier than anticipated, and we haven't detected the three-tiered[9] cloud structure that our researchers had expected. The amount of helium measured is about one-half of what the statistics showed.

"Shuttle 01. You are now on course. Everything's looking good. You are set for go."

"Aye, aye, Sir! We are entering Pelleus's atmosphere. There seem to be some gravitational disturbances, Sir. The shuttle is vibrating. The plasma detection module is registering strong winds and very intense subspace shock waves."

This could mean that the energy source driving much of the planet's circulation phenomena is probably heat escaping from its deep interior.

"Ready for touch-down! We go for landing."

---

8 interference – *Störung*

9 three-tiered – *aus drei Schichten bestehend*

**00:22 in mission**

"This is Shuttle 01. The shuttle has landed, Sir!"

We are on the surface of Pelleus! I am working on the BDS (biosphere-detection-scanner). The readings suggest that Pelleus has a bulk composition similar to that of the gas and dust cloud of the primitive solar nebula from which the planets and our Sun were formed, with added heavy elements from comets and meteorites.

What is that? The scanner alarm signals the presence of a solid object hidden in the dust and at the centre of a magnetic field, about half a mile from where we are.

**00:32 in mission**

"What do you make of it?" Angus wants to know.

"The only way to find out is to look for ourselves! Ready for EVA (extra-vehicular-activity)!"

Commander Kerry, Angus and the android Jules are leaving the shuttle to investigate the matter.

**00:53 in mission**

The waiting is terrible. I hate it! Then Angus' voice over the intercom: "Hey, Dave!" He sounds excited and he is breathing heavily. "We've got to the site. You'll never guess what we found. One of our –!"

"Commander Kerry! Your report!" demands an impatient Captain Sandrew.

"Sir, the object emitting radio signals is Investigation Starship Hercules. It is on the ground here. How on earth it got here, I don't know. There's nobody around.

Dust is blowing all over the place. Shall we try to enter the ship, Sir?"

"Kerry, I'm still puzzled about the loss of radio contact on your descent[1]. There's something strange happening here! Kerry, you have permission to enter, but watch out. Have your phaser-guns ready!"

"Aye, aye, Sir, we're going in!"

**01:12 in mission**

"Hey, Angus! What's going on. Tell me!"

"This is Commander Kerry for Captain Sandrew! Sir, we've found seventeen astronauts aboard ISS Hercules. They are all in bad shape. Out of their crew of twenty-four five are dead, two are missing. Multiple hits from laser cannons have seriously damaged the craft. The ship is not manoeuvrable. Computer and radio transmitter are dead or damaged, as are most of the other systems. The only transmitter still working is the UDT (Ultimate Danger Transmitter). That's where the radio signals we picked up came from.

Sir, somebody or something has put the energy supply system into reverse and has re-programmed it on a self-destruction date. The spacecraft could explode any minute!"

"Commander Kerry! More trouble on the way! An unidentified object is approaching your position on an intercept[2] course. You'd better leave the ship immediately!"

1 descent – *Abstieg*
2 to intercept – *abfangen*

"Sir, our only chance is for Dave to activate evacuation systems in Shuttle 01 and get us out as quickly as possible!"

Captain's voice: "Lieutenant Vandenberg, did you hear that?"

"Yes, Sir."

"And you know what that means?"

"EVA, Sir. I'm on my way out!"

In order to activate the security shield and turn the small shuttle into an evacuation craft the thrusters[3] outside need to be repositioned manually. In the dust storm a difficult task to perform. I've never tried that before.

Angus: "Good luck, Dave – and, please, hurry up. We haven't got much time left!"

**01:21 in mission**

I'm trying to perform a miracle. I'm outside. It's hard to climb along the ship. Last time I did some climbing exercise was on Valera 4.

I'm beginning to sweat in my survival suit. I'm receiving mysterious signals from an unknown source. Have the aliens located me?

The thrusters! Thank God, I can see them through the dust cloud. Now, find the right position so that the thrusters can be fired manually! Done! Ugh!

"Sir. This is Shuttle 01. Thrusters in position!"

I think I can hear some hands clapping in the background, or am I just imagining it?!

---

3 thrust – *Schub; hier: Antriebsaggregat*

Captain's voice: "Well done, Dave! An unidentified spacecraft is approaching fast! Get away quickly!"

**01:30 in mission**

I'm inside again. The computer is programmed to the position of ISS Hercules, I have set the engine burn to 26 seconds. Now, let's hope the thrusters don't let me down. The engines fire! Good old superpropulsion!! The security shield is up! I'm taking Shuttle 01 over to rescue those survivors on Hercules!

**01:52 in mission**

Jules has been working like a maniac. We have recovered all the bodies from ISS Hercules. Everybody's aboard Shuttle 01 – now an evacuation craft – except for Commander Kerry and Angus.

"Twenty-five seconds left to get ourselves on a link course to Equity!"

"Commander Kerry! Angus! Where are you!"

Hurry up. Where have they gone? At last! Here they come, dragging[4] behind them a wounded crew member. The last one.

"Lieutenant Vandenberg! Launch the shuttle! Activate thrusters and leave that infamous[5] site at once!"

"Yes, Sir, Captain!"

Everybody's on board. Here we go! We have lift off!

4 to drag – *schleppen*
5 infamous – *abscheulich*

**02 : 02 in mission**

The reflection of a red fire ball exploding on the very spot we have just left turns the inside of our vehicle yellow-red. That was close! The enemy ship had fired a photon torpedo and destroyed the Hercules.

**02 : 20 in mission**

Mission completed. We have re-docked to Equity.
Congratulations for me from the Captain and all the crew!

Everybody is glad that our excursion has ended safely, although none of us understands what really happened to the ISS Hercules, why we lost radio contact etc.

Our chief science engineer tries to explain, "In my view we lost the emergency distress[6] signal because ..."

"Excuse, me, Sir. The communication sensors are picking up a message coming in on the language translation responder."

"Activate the translation module."

We listen to a dark resounding voice:

"Humans! We want you to clearly understand this message. Listen closely to what we, the Cheviots people, have to tell you. Your investigation vessel had invaded our territory. We tried to destroy the craft, not because we are a hostile nation, no, but because we have been studying your planet and its customs from computer data and videos of your television broadcasts. We abhor[7] your cruelties, your hostilities and your wars. In our world we do not raise our children to see them being killed off in senseless warfare. That is why we want to be left alone. We want to stay in our splendid isolation. We do not want to be discovered by you and become yet another member of your Colonial Star System. We do not want your pioneers to bring diseases. We do not want you to exploit our resources, nor corrupt our customs and way of life! We do not want you to ruthlessly slaughter[8] our population. Make no mistake about our determination. You may

---

6 distress – *Not*

7 to abhor – *verabscheuen*

8 slaughter – *(ab)schlachten*

travel home now, humans – but do not dare come back!"

Nobody says a word, we are stunned and embarrassed.

The Captain is the first to speak.

"Well, there certainly is truth in what their leader says. Maybe this is not the only place where we are not welcome! It's perhaps time for us to re-think our policy of expansion."

"Reminds me of good old Kant a bit."

"Who? What are you talking about, Angus?"

"Kant. Immanuel Kant. German philosopher of the 18th century. *'Act as if the maxim of your action were to become through your will a general natural law.'* That's what he said in his categorical imperative."

"O my God, I didn't know you were a philosopher, Angus!"

"I'm not, Dave. But it does make me think when people don't want to be detected by us because they don't think ours is the best form of civilization. They don't want us to interfere with them."

"Now let's go back to our quarters. We both have a lot of sleep to catch up with!"

The voice of the first officer over the intercom: "Lieutenants MacPherson and Vandenberg to the shuttle bay at once!"

## The Day the President was Killed

Normally I do not talk about my job to anyone. If I carry out my duties properly nobody notices that I'm there. What I have done all my life has gone on unnoticed behind the scenes. My job is – or rather was – to protect people, not film stars or pop singers, but important politicians working for the government in Washington. That protection also includes their families, especially their children until they are sixteen years old. The Service I have worked for is also responsible for the personal security of foreign heads of state when they visit the US, for example Queen Elizabeth and her husband. In short, we protect people who are in danger of being attacked by some terrorist or maniac[1]. If all goes well, then nobody talks about us, but if a tragedy happens like in 1963 ...! I shall never forget that most terrible and frightening experience of my working life. I felt so helpless, frustrated and sad. Now that I am about to retire from the Service I can tell you the story of what happened the day President John F. Kennedy was assassinated[2].

***

1 maniac – *Wahnsinniger, (gefährlicher) Verrückter*
2 to assassinate – *ermorden*

I was 31 then and I had been an agent with the FBI for four years. We are an 'FBI-family' you might say, because both my grandfather Bert and my father Ben were FBI agents. Granddad Bert was even one of the pioneers of the 'Federal Bureau of Investigation'. He joined the Bureau in 1924. That was the time when J. Edgar Hoover became the first director of the agency. Hoover stayed for 48 years in that top position. In the thirties it was decided the FBI would take over some work areas of the normal police forces of the individual states. In cases of espionage, sabotage, and organized crime the Bureau would take control of investigations. By the way, the agency was given its name 'FBI' as late as 1935.

So it was quite clear to me from the beginning that I wanted to be an FBI agent, too. As soon as I graduated[3] from George Washington University I handed in my application at the FBI's national headquarters in Washington, D.C. I received the normal training and then worked in the Identification Division where we study and classify fingerprints. Naturally, I attended courses which informed us about the latest crime-detection methods: How to analyse traces[4] of dust, paint, glass, and other evidence[5] that can only be seen under a microscope. I was quite a good agent, I must admit, and my father was very proud of me. In order to complete my training I applied to take part in a special

3 to graduate – *(Am. E.) von der Hochschule abgehen*
4 trace – *Spur*
5 evidence – *Beweis*

program which was run by the Secret Service in Washington about the personal protection of VIPs, that is to say 'Very Important Persons'.

You have to know that the Secret Service in Washington was started as a division of the Department of the Treasury[6]! Their job there was to investigate cases of forgery[7], which means to arrest people who tried to print dollars. Over the years, however, the agency became responsible for the personal protection of the president, the vice president and their families. The agents of the Secret Service do not only protect the politicians while they are working in their offices in Washington, but 24 hours a day. Wherever the president, his wife or their children go, agents accompany them everywhere around the clock. When the president welcomes the British prime minister or the German chancellor at the White House, the agents are there. When his wife wants to do some private shopping in Washington, the agents go with her. When his children want to go to a friend's birthday party, the Secret Service agents have to be informed about this event in advance[8], so that they can check the security without disturbing the families and the children too much. They go to the house where the party takes place and they check everything to guarantee the safety of the President's son or daughter.

---

6 Department of the Treasury – *amerik. Finanzministerium*
7 forgery – *Fälschung*
8 in advance – *im Voraus*

***

So on November 1, 1963, I reported for work in Washington, D.C. and walked into the office of Special Agent Winston G. Lawson. He was sitting behind his desk and before I could say anything he greeted me with, "Hello, morning, son! You're just in time to take a little trip with me to Texas!"

"Good morning, Sir", I replied. "I'm afraid there must be a mistake. I'm supposed to . . ."

"Oh, no, young man. There's no mistake. We don't make mistakes in here," he laughed.

"I know who you are, what you're here for, and for next couple of weeks or so you'll be working with me," added my new boss.

Before I could say anything else, Lawson carried on, "We're off to Dallas tomorrow!"

"Why Dallas, Sir?" Then the agent told me about the President's plans for a visit to the state of Texas.

I had never met President John F. Kennedy in person before. I only knew him and his beautiful wife, Jacqueline Lee Bouvier, from television and the papers like everybody else I suppose. Well, like any good pupil at school I remembered that in 1960 he had won the presidential elections against his rival from the Republican Party, Richard M. Nixon. At 43 the Democrat Kennedy was one of the youngest men ever to be elected president of the USA. On tour in Germany he had won the hearts of millions of Germans when he said the sentence "Ich bin ein Berliner".

I also knew that some Conservatives didn't like his plans for tax reform which would mean that the rich had to pay higher taxes and the poor less. The President felt great sympathy for Martin Luther King and his work, and that is why Kennedy planned to give more civil rights to African-Americans. He was very popular with the younger generation, because they thought he would lead them on their way to a new America.

Lawson told me that President Kennedy had not been to Texas for some time, and that there was a political reason for his visit to this southern state.

"I'm sure, the President has the coming elections of 1964 in mind. He is aware of not being popular in Texas, but he also knows that he needs the votes of the Texans badly. That's why he wants to go down there with his wife to show himself to the crowds. A sort of public relations[9] journey. And, above all, the President likes to meet the American people. When he can talk to people personally he learns first-hand about their problems and worries. In a way it is like being a film star. He has always enjoyed appearing in public and so he is looking forward to the visit."

"So does all this mean that we have to organise the President's visit to Texas?" I asked.

"Not quite. A lot has already been done for us in Dallas by the local police there and our FBI office. I have just received a message from the office of the Texan Governor Connally for us to come down and discuss the final details of the visit."

Early next morning – almost in the middle of the night, I thought – we flew to Love Field Airport, Dallas in a special military plane. George Swiggart, one of our FBI representatives down there, came to collect[10] us. At 9:15 a.m. we drove to Dallas Headquarters to meet a number of police officers and Secret Service agents. We wanted to go through the security arrangements for the day of the President's visit which was now scheduled[11] for Friday, November 22.

"Everyone knows how much the President wants to be seen and make contact with the people on this special trip. That doesn't make our job easy, folks. Anyway, we are sure that the best way for the people to see

9 public relations – *Öffentlichkeitsarbeit*
10 to collect – *hier: jmdn. abholen*
11 to schedule – *planen, vorsehen*

their President is to arrange a motorcade through the centre of Dallas," Lawson said.

"A motorcade?" exclaimed the Chief of Police.

The FBI agent explained, "Yeah. A motorcade. You know, a number of cars and motorcycles drive through the main streets, with the President and his wife Jackie in the middle car."

"That's a good idea, Winston", the Chief of Police went on. "Police motorcycles can lead the way, followed by the so-called pilot car. Then we'll have more motorbikes and the lead car, in which the agents will be sitting. About four or five car-lengths behind them will be the President's limousine. We'll put two more motorcycles on each side to keep back the crowds. Then the follow-up car with more Secret Service agents. Finally the cars with the rest of the party."

The Police Chief cleared his throat[12] before continuing.

"This is what I suggest for the motorcade. Altogether we'll have 45 minutes for the drive from the airport through the town to the Trade Mart building. That is the place where the President will deliver a speech and have lunch with important businessmen. We shall select a route of about 4 miles which can be driven easily within that time."

"What about the security in the Trade Mart building?" Lawson asked.

"Wait a minute, Winston. I'll finish with the route first. So, the President will arrive at Love Field airport

12 to clear one's throat – *sich räuspern*

From there he, Jackie and Governor Connally and his wife will travel in the Presidential limousine, a specially equipped Lincoln. There will be no stops on the way."

"And what happens if the President wants to stop?" one of the officers at the back asked.

"If the President orders a stop to greet the crowds, you Secret Service people have to move as quickly as possible. When the motorcade slows or stops, agents must take positions between the President and the crowd. To make it easier for you, we'll choose a route with wide streets. We'll have enough room then between the people who want to see the President and the President's car."

"What about tall buildings, bridges, overpasses[13] on the way?" Lawson asked.

"We must carefully check the roofs of buildings, overpasses, and crossings on the route to be sure it is safe. This afternoon we'll drive through Dallas with you to put you in the picture. Now then, as to security measures at the Trade Mart building. Agent Beck will tell you all about that."

A tall dark-haired agent rose, and said. "As soon as we were told that the Trade Mart had been selected for the President's luncheon speech we have been working on security arrangements at the building. On the day of the President's visit we'll have absolute control of people who wish to enter the building. We shall close off the area and policemen and agents in plain

---

13 overpass – *Überführung*

clothes[14] will patrol the area around it. All in all, more than 200 officers and Secret Agents will be in and around the Trade Mart."

After the meeting we spent a very busy afternoon and night in Dallas. We drove along the route, went into the Trade Mart building, talked to the local police if they had any information about political trouble-makers in the town, inspected the cars that would be used in the motorcade etc. etc. We checked everything. When I fell into bed that night, I was completely exhausted, but I was quite satisfied that we had done a good job. We were convinced that we could guarantee the security of the President. We didn't know then, of course, how terribly wrong we were to be!

***

Friday, November 22, 1963 started as a rainy and unfriendly day in Dallas, Texas. By midmorning, however, we were all pleased when the rain stopped and the sun came out shining brightly. I was among the Service Agents at Love Field and watched the President's special plane, Air Force One, coming in to land at 11:40 a.m. The Texan Governor Connally, his wife Nellie and other important politicians were there to welcome the President with red roses and asters. Among the welcome committee was also Vice President Lyndon B. Johnson, who – for security reasons –

---

14 plain clothes – *in Zivil(kleidung)*

had travelled in a different plane, Air Force Two, and who had arrived just a few minutes earlier.

A large crowd of Kennedy fans was shouting and cheering at the airport. For security reasons they were kept back behind chain-link fences[15]. As I had learned how much the President loved meeting and talking to people, I turned to Lawson and said, "I bet you five dollars that he'll walk over to talk to them." Before Lawson had any chance of accepting or refusing my bet, sure enough, President Kennedy had walked over to the spectators behind the fence. He and his wife spent five minutes shaking hands and chatting before they went to their automobile. Then the drive into Dallas, the motorcade, began.

Lawson and I jumped into the lead car. The President's limousine followed about four or five car-lengths behind. Like all the other agents I carried a 38-caliber pistol, and I knew that Lawson had seen to it that we also had a shotgun and an automatic rifle in our car. I'm sure you will realize that we thought we had done everything possible to protect the President!

As the weather was fine, the personal advisors of the President had decided that he would travel in an open-top car. They knew, of course, how much he would like that. It was now shortly after 11:50 a.m. and we drove at a speed of about 25 miles per hour into Dallas. In the outskirts[16] there were already quite a few people along the streets and the President told his driver to

---

15 fence – *Zaun, Absperrung*
16 outskirts – *Außenbezirke, Vororte*

stop twice. He wanted to shake hands with somebody and talk to a Catholic nun and a group of small children. As soon as his limousine stopped agents from the follow-up car came forward and stood beside the President's car, looking out toward the crowd.

Everything had gone well so far. When we reached the downtown area I noticed that there were more and more people who wanted to catch a glimpse[17] of the President and his wife Jackie. Now and then the motorcade had to slow down because of the masses of spectators. I got quite a shock when I saw a young boy running towards the President's car, but Special Agent John D. Ready stopped the little one and told him to go back onto the sidewalk[18] again.

Driving at about 11 miles per hour our car turned into Elm Street toward the Triple Underpass. The time was exactly 12:30. I remember it so clearly because I noticed that the large clock on the top of the Texas School Book Depository Building showed the numerals '12:30'. I had a look at my own watch and thought it was two minutes slow.

The President and Governor Connally seemed very pleased about the friendly reception. Mrs Nellie Connally turned to President Kennedy and said, "Mr President, you can't say Dallas doesn't love you." The President replied, "That is very obvious."

"We should be at the Trade Mart building by now", Lawson said to me. "But, not to worry, it's only a cou-

---

17 to catch a glimpse – *einen Blick erhaschen*
18 sidewalk – *(Am. E.) Bürgersteig*

ple of minutes from here." I was just about to ask him exactly what time he made it when I heard a loud bang. At first I thought it was a firecracker or a backfire from one of the motorcycles. But it wasn't! A shot had been fired!

Then a thousand things happened at the same time. "Oh, my God!" someone screamed. "He's been shot! Oh, no! No!" I saw Mrs Kennedy, who sat on the left of the rear seat of the limousine, turn to her husband. The President moved his left hand to his neck. There was a cry from Governor Connally. I heard another shot approximately 5 seconds after the first. The bullet hit the President's head. He fell to his left. Blood ran from his skull[19].

I looked up at the seven-story Texas School Book Building, a warehouse for textbooks, and I still think that I saw a man withdrawing[20] from a window on the sixth floor. I'll never be able to prove that, though.

Kennedy's brave driver, William Greer, reacted quickly. As it had been laid out in our plans in case of an emergency he quickly pulled out of the motorcade. At 70 m.p.h. he rushed down the highway to get away from the scene. Lawson took the radio telephone and called the police escorts ahead. "Let's get out of here. The President is hit. Get us to the nearest hospital immediately!"

I saw how Secret Service man Clinton J. Hill, who had travelled in the car following the President, ran along the road and jumped onto the President's limousine to help Mrs Kennedy. She had started to climb onto the back of the car. Everywhere security agents shouted, "Get down! Get down!" All cars picked up speed and raced after the Presidential limousine down the Stemmons Freeway.

***

19 skull – *Schädel*
20 to withdraw – *sich zurückziehen*

Five minutes later, all cars arrived almost simultaneously at the emergency entrance of Parkland Memorial Hospital. Mrs Kennedy was still holding her husband, her skirt and stockings were full of blood.

"Get some stretchers[21]!" Together with three other agents I ran inside the hospital. The President and Governor Connally were taken into the emergency room where doctors were already waiting. Vice-President Lyndon Johnson thought he was having a heart attack. He was all right though, just deeply shocked – like all the rest of us. Admiral Burkley, the President's personal doctor, arrived at the hospital about three minutes later. The driver of his car had not realized what had happened and had gone on to the Trade Mart first.

We stationed several policemen at the entrance of the hospital, as more and more people started to arrive. They were all shocked and wanted to know how seriously the President was wounded. Police and Secret Service agents tried their best to keep the public and press away from the hospital. The dreadful waiting began.

Shortly after 1 p.m. there were rumours among the agents that President Kennedy had died of his severe head injury. 12 doctors had tried to save his life – but in vain! The unthinkable had happened! Some maniac had killed the most important and most powerful man in the Western world. When I was told the news, I

---

21 stretchers – *Tragbahre*

just stood there – completely stunned[22] by what had happened. I couldn't help it, but tears were running down my face. I started weeping! As I'm telling you all this, I still get rather emotional. All those memories are coming back to me!

***

There was not much time for mourning[23], however. We, the security forces and police officers, were busier than ever. Our job as Secret Service agents was now to protect the Vice President and Mrs Johnson. We led Lyndon Johnson to a room in the hospital. "You stay right here at the entrance, son," Lawson told me. "Don't let anybody pass who is not a member of the President's staff!" A number of special agents were sent back to the scene of the assassination to hunt the killer. All this happened about 20 or 25 minutes after the shots were fired in Elm Street.

Special Agent Youngblood asked Mrs Johnson where her two daughters were at the moment. In a few minutes the girls would be the daughters of the new US President! Mrs Johnson said they were in Washington. Youngblood phoned the Secret Service headquarters and ordered them to provide extra protection for the girls immediately.

---

22 stunned – *wie betäubt*
23 to mourn – *trauern*

It was decided that the death of John F. Kennedy should not be announced to the press straight away. Secret Service agents insisted that Vice President Johnson should return to Washington first on the Presidential plane, Air Force One. Johnson waited for Mrs Kennedy. The dead body of JFK was put in a coffin and loaded onto the plane. Still on the ground in Dallas Lyndon Baines Johnson took the Presidential oath of office[24] as the 36th President of the United States, with Mrs Kennedy in her pink blood-stained[25] costume standing beside him.

Police and Secret Service agents started to track down the assassin. On the sixth floor of the schoolbook warehouse detectives discovered left-overs of a chicken dinner in a bag, an empty soft drinks bottle, and three empty cartridge[26] cases. The killer, however, was gone.

Some time later a man named Lee Harvey Oswald was arrested. When police took him to another building to be interrogated[27] he was shot by a nightclub owner called Jack Ruby, and so Oswald could never be tried in court[28].

What followed were speculations about the question "Did Oswald really shoot the President?", "Did he act alone or was it a conspiracy[29]?", "Who had an interest

---

24 oath of office – *Amtseid*
25 stain – *Fleck*
26 cartridge – *Patrone*
27 to interrogate – *verhören*
28 to try in court – *vor Gericht stellen*
29 conspiracy – *Verschwörung, Komplott*

in President Kennedy's death?", "Was the Mafia behind the murder?"

Over the past decades hundreds of books have been written about what happened that day in Dallas, Texas. But books, films and videos cannot give you the same impression that I personally experienced when I think back to Friday, November 22, 1963.

## King Arthur and Queen Guinevere

The days of great King Arthur lie buried deep in the mists of time. Through the centuries men and women of all ages have passed on the legends of the famous 'Knights of the Round Table' to younger generations. The adventures of King Arthur and his knights are stories of bravery, courage and honesty. They are also shining ideals of gallant behaviour to ladies, of unrequited love[1] and devotion[2]. That is why the legends live on ...

In the dark ages of unrest and conflict in Britain, after the fall of the Roman Empire, Arthur and his wise helper, the magician Merlin, came to the rescue of their country. The mysterious Lady of the Lake gave young Arthur a magic sword: 'Excalibur'. With it he was invincible[3] and fought fearlessly against invaders from north and east. Many bold noblemen helped him to battle against the 'barbarians' and also against rebels in his own country.

Arthur did not command a big army, but he was clever and nearly always took his enemies by surprise. He never gave his opponents any chance of knowing where and when he would attack. When the rebels

---

1 unrequited love – *nicht erwiderte Liebe*
2 devotion – *Hingabe*
3 invincible – *unbesiegbar*

thought that he was far away engaged in some battle, Arthur and his loyal followers would pounce[4] suddenly from out of the woods. It took seven long years before victory was achieved. In the end, the invaders were driven off the island and the rebels promised to keep peace.

4 to pounce – *hervorstürzen; sich stürzen*

The people in Britain were relieved that after so many years of suffering and destruction peace had at last returned. They all knew that the man they had to thank for this was Arthur. So at a meeting that no one was ever to forget, the noblemen of Britain made Arthur their King.

***

The young King decided to set up his court at the castle of Camelot. On his way back to Camelot, he passed through Camelerede, where his friend Leodegraunce had his castle. Arthur stopped there to stay for the night. His men were exhausted and badly needed a rest before they carried on their journey.

When the knights sat together feasting and talking about old times, Arthur met the beautiful daughter of Leodegraunce for the first time. Her name was Guinevere, and for Arthur it was love at first sight. He knew immediately that Guinevere was the woman he wanted to spend the rest of his days with. She should be his Queen, not only of his heart, but of his kingdom, too.

Arthur did not tell anyone about his secret thoughts. He knew that he had to talk to Merlin, the wizard[5], first. Merlin had always been his helper and adviser, he would know best what to do and how to win Guinevere's love.

---

5 wizard, magician – *Zauberer*

"Merlin, now that peace has returned to the country, I think it is time for me to get married. I have met the sweetest and fairest maiden in the world and I want her to be my queen."

Merlin was not surprised at Arthur's words. "Who is she?" he asked in a low voice. He sounded rather disinterested as if he knew the answer already.

"Her name is Guinevere, she is the daughter of King Leodegraunce and the most beautiful woman I have ever seen…" Arthur's cheeks turned red with excitement as he kept telling Merlin about Guinevere's beauty and charm. He was completely carried away and did not notice that Merlin had become very quiet. The magician did not seem to be listening at all. He gazed into the distance, looking rather sad.

"Hey, what is wrong with you, Merlin?! Aren't you pleased about my plans? Aren't you looking forward to a royal wedding?"

"O Arthur, I am pleased that you have decided to get married."

"But you don't look it, Merlin. You give me the impression as if you had just been told that the sun would not rise any more."

"I wished indeed, Arthur, that you had chosen some other princess."

"Honestly, Merlin! I can't believe what you are saying. Guinevere is the most wonderful person in the world. For me there is no one like her."

"I know that, Arthur. I know you have set your mind on marrying Guinevere and there is no turning back. However, your love will not be a happy one. Your

love is doomed[6]. Guinevere's beauty will cause problems at your court. She will bring jealousy and strife[7] between you and your best friends – and eventually she will bring about the end of Camelot. Her very beauty has bewitched[8] you, Arthur. But what good does it do to tell you all that? You think that she is the fairest princess in the world."

"That's right, Merlin. You are getting a bit old! And the older you get the stranger you talk. I do not want to listen to what you are saying about the future. I'm asking you to go to Guinevere's father and tell him that I want to marry his beautiful daughter."

So Merlin went to King Leo and told him about Arthur's love and his plans. Leodegraunce was very pleased, and the wedding was arranged for Whitsun. Thousands of people turned up to attend the royal wedding ceremony and were overjoyed at the sight of the handsome royal couple. Afterwards tournaments[9] were held in which many noble knights fought against each other to entertain the crowds.

---

6 doomed – *zum Scheitern verurteilt*
7 jealousy and strife – *Eifersucht und Streit*
8 bewitched – *verhext (witch = Hexe)*
9 tournament – *Turnier*

***

On the seventh day an unknown knight arrived. He did not wear any colours and did not want to give his name. Fighting on behalf of[10] the lovely Queen Guinevere, he defeated the best and strongest knights in the tournament, and the people started asking themselves who this man might be. The stranger at last revealed his identity.

10 on behalf of – *für, im Namen*

"My lord Arthur", he said, "my name is Lancelot du Lac. I have come from across the sea. I have come to Camelot to be knighted and to serve at your court." As champion of the tournament Lancelot was knighted. This event marked the beginning of a great friendship between these two excellent men. Neither of them had any idea, however, that their love for the same wonderful lady Guinevere was eventually to bring hatred, destruction and death.

After the celebrations Arthur worked hard to govern his kingdom. In the evenings there was time for feasting and singing. The knights and their ladies, the dancers and musicians assembled in the Great Hall. The enormous room was lit by flaming torches which were fixed on the walls. The stone walls were decorated with valuable tapestries[11] showing wild animals and scenes of tournaments and hunting. In the middle of the hall there stood a great round table, made of oak, with finely carved[12] chairs arranged around it. Guinevere had brought this wonderful table with her as her wedding present. The name of each knight was carved in letters of gold on the back of every seat. The table was round because its shape was a symbol of the equality[13] of the knights: Nobody's seat was ahead of or below anyone else's.

---

11 tapestry – *Gobelin, Wandteppich*
12 to carve – *schnitzen*
13 equality – *Gleichheit*

***

It had always been Arthur's wish to gather the bravest and most honourable knights of the known world at his court. That is why he proclaimed[14] the 'Fellowship of the Knights of the Round Table': "Let us solemnly swear to be gallant and chivalrous[15]. Let us promise to assist anyone who comes to us in need of help. Let us defend the weak. We shall destroy the evil forces that endanger peace in the country! Once a year we shall meet here at Camelot and tell each other of our adventures!"

One chair at the large table was left empty. It was called the 'Siège Perilous' and was reserved for the perfect knight who had not yet been born. The years passed by and the Knights of the Round Table participated in lots of adventures and won great victories. Throughout the country they were respected and loved by the weak and poor, but they were feared by the mean and evil[16]. The celebrated warriors brought peace to the land. However, they had to pay a high price: Many knights were killed or died of their wounds. Over the years some chairs at the Round Table had become empty.

One knight stood out from all the others: it was Lancelot. He was in more battles and he won more tournaments than any other cavalier. In lowly homes

---

14 proclaim – *ausrufen*
15 chivalrous – *ritterlich*
16 evil – *schlecht, böse*

and in magnificent castles people told stories of his amazing adventures, praising his courage and skill.

Lancelot still loved and admired the beautiful and gentle Queen Guinevere. He wore her colours at tournaments, and always kept the thought of the noble and lovely lady in his mind.

With the passing of time people noticed how often Lancelot and Guinevere were together. There were many rumours about a love affair between the Queen and King Arthur's best and finest knight. Arthur himself did not suspect that his wife would be unfaithful[17]. He thought that there was nothing wrong in the best knight at his court fighting on behalf of the Queen.

The happy days slowly came to an end, and Merlin's words about the end of Camelot were about to become true.

***

Among the many fine knights in Arthur's kingdom there were also a few evil and vicious[18] ones. The leader of these evil knights was Mordred, Arthur's nephew. He was jealous of Arthur and wanted to become king himself. To satisfy his ambition[19] Mordred worked out a plan to destroy[20] the Brotherhood

---

17 unfaithful – *untreu, treulos*
18 vicious – *bösartig, gemein*
19 ambition – *Ehrgeiz*
20 destroy – *zerstören*

of the Round Table and the friendship between Arthur and Lancelot. Mordred knew that Lancelot and Guinevere were in love with each other. So he sent out spies[21] to watch the couple. Lancelot was clever enough to realize that he was being followed. The next time he met Guinevere in the garden of the royal palace he told her:

"My Queen, I am afraid our situation has become dangerous, but we cannot talk here and now. Too many eyes are watching us and too many ears are listening in."

"Come then to my room tonight and tell me more", Guinevere answered.

Mordred's spies overheard[22] this conversation and told him about it. Mordred went straight to Arthur to arouse[23] his jealousy.

"Guinevere and Lancelot are meeting in the Queen's chamber tonight!"

"Liar! That's not true!" Arthur shouted.

"If you want proof, see for yourself tonight."

Arthur hesitated[24]. He thought it unfair to spy on his wife in such an underhand[25] manner. He would rather have talked to Guinevere and Lancelot frankly. But eventually Mordred persuaded him to come along. They hid in the palace and when night came they saw Lancelot hurrying along the corridor. He stopped in

---

21 spy – *Spion*
22 to overhear – *belauschen*
23 to arouse – *wecken*
24 hesitate – *zögern*
25 underhand – *hinterhältig, verschlagen*

front of the Queen's quarters, and knocked at the door. At once the door was opened and Lancelot disappeared into the room.

"You see, I've told you the truth, my noble King. Lancelot and Guinevere are traitors[1]. You must have them arrested immediately!" Mordred urged[2] Arthur.

The King was so shocked and disappointed that he could not say anything. So Mordred took advantage of the King's helplessness and shouted aloud to his followers: "Break into the room! Arrest the traitors!"

Lancelot had become aware of the noise going on outside. When he heard Mordred's commanding voice, he drew his sword, fought his way out and managed to escape.

***

Mordred insisted that Guinevere should be treated like all traitors: she should be burned at the stake[3]. Although Guinevere assured Arthur of her loyalty, the King did not seem to listen to what she was saying. He had fallen into some kind of apathy[4]. He did not seem to care much about what was happening. His world had come to an end. He watched sadly as wood was being piled up in the yard to prepare a stake for Guinevere to be burnt.

1 traitor – *Verräter*
2 to urge – *drängen*
3 stake – *Scheiterhaufen*
4 apathy – *Teilnahmslosigkeit*

The following morning – darkness had just lifted – the unhappy Queen was led to the stake. Rough hands grabbed her and tied her to a post. A torch was brought along to light the wood. At the very moment when the first flames glowed knights mounted on white horses galloped into the square. It was Lancelot and his followers. They attacked and killed several guards, cut Guinevere free and rescued her.

Hearing the clanging of swords and shouts of men below King Arthur came to his senses again. Deep inside he was glad that Guinevere's life had been saved, but he also knew that he now had to take on Lancelot and fight against him.

Moreover, one of the knights that Lancelot had killed in the attack was Gawain's brother. Gawain, one of the bravest and best knights at the Round Table, wanted Arthur to fight against Lancelot to revenge[5] the death of his brother.

Many fierce[6] battles between Arthur's and Lancelot's armies were fought and many brave knights lost their lives. The Brotherhood of the Round Table had ended in bloodshed[7]. Lancelot wanted to put an end to the killings, so he brought Guinevere back to Arthur, hoping that with her return to her husband the fighting would be over. Lancelot himself left Britain and sailed back to France.

---

5 revenge – *rächen, Rache*
6 fierce – *heftig*
7 bloodshed – *Blutvergießen*

***

Gawain, who had lost his brother, could not forgive or forget what had happened. He was still full of hatred against Lancelot and kept pressing Arthur to lead an army against his brother's slayer[8].

"My King, you must not sit here and let that traitor get away with murder. The souls of those brave knights of yours that he killed cry to me every night. Revenge, revenge! This is what they want! Arthur, let us cross the water and go into France and find Lancelot! We owe this to our Brothers of the Round Table."

Gawain finally succeeded in persuading the King. Arthur agreed to start on an expedition to France to look for Lancelot and kill him. He decided, unwisely, that while he and Gawain were away his nephew Mordred should rule the country.

This was the chance Mordred had been waiting for: He could at last become king of Britain! Arthur and Gawain had hardly left for the coast to sail across the Channel when Mordred and his men spread the news that Arthur was dead: "Arthur is dead. I am now your King!"

Loyal friends informed Guinevere of Mordred's plans, and the Queen managed to flee to London, together with a few loyal servants. She despised Mordred and sent a faithful messenger to Arthur and

8 to slay – *erschlagen*

Gawain to inform them of Mordred's treachery[9]. As soon as the two received the message they returned to England. Mordred and his men were waiting for them at Dover to prevent Arthur from entering the country.

***

One of the most dreadful battles ever to be fought on English soil began. It lasted a whole day and only stopped when many noble knights lay dead on the cold ground. When evening fell, the silence of death spread[10] over the battlefield. Arthur wept when he saw that most of his followers had been killed.

9 treachery – *Verrat*
10 to spread – *sich ausbreiten*

"Oh God! What has become of all my noble knights. Oh had I never seen this sad day! There lies brave Gawain. But where is that scoundrel[11] who started all this? The man responsible for the deaths of these brave brothers? Where is that traitor Mordred?"

Hardly had Arthur spoken these words when he saw Mordred galloping across the field over the dead bodies like a maniac. Arthur rushed at the traitor, but his sword-belt came loose and his sword Excalibur fell to the ground. Mordred put all his hate and fury into his fight with the King. Gripping his sword with both hands he hit Arthur upon the head so hard that the blade[12] cut through the helmet and deep into the skull. At the same time Mordred received a fatal[13] blow himself and fell to the ground screaming.

Arthur was badly wounded. He had fallen at the hands of the Evil Knight. Knowing his time had come, he turned to the last survivor of his faithful knights, Sir Bedevere, "Bedevere, help me to get to the lake beyond those hills before I die! Find Excalibur, too!"

Arthur remembered the words the Lady of the Lake had spoken to him such a long time ago: "When your time has come to die, Arthur, you must come back to the lake and bring the sword I now put into your hands with you. It must be returned to the water, the element from which it came. If you don't do this no one will ever remember your name."

---

11 scoundrel – *Schurke*
12 blade – *Klinge*
13 fatal – *tödlich*

Arriving at the misty lake a boat was already waiting for the dying Arthur. In it were four ladies who tended to[14] his wounds and glided with him over the water back to Avalon, the enchanted land of eternal spring. Arthur was never seen again.

When Lancelot heard the news that Mordred had betrayed Arthur, he was so incensed that he set out for Britain to fight for the rightful King. But on his arrival he learned that it was too late: Arthur had disappeared somewhere in the west country and had not been seen for more than a month. Lancelot found a heartbroken Guinevere, who gently refused his offer of protection. She spent the rest of her days in a convent[15], and Lancelot went to live in a monastery. Arthur's court at Camelot and the Knights of the Round Table had ceased to exist.

14 to tend to – *(Wunden) pflegen*
15 convent, monastery – *Kloster*

*(Bitte blättern Sie um)*